Praise for THE LONG BLINK

During my more than fifty-year career in television news, I have worked with an endless number of reporters. Some have been excellent storytellers. Some of their stories have made a significant difference. Brian Kuebler's *The Long Blink* is the rare combination of both.

Kuebler is one of this country's most persistent and dedicated investigative reporters whose writing eloquently animates some of the most important stories of our time. Once he met Ed Slattery, once he learned how Slattery's family was left broken forever by a tired truck driver, Kuebler not only saw an issue on our roads, but also a gripping personal story of tragedy and loss that helps restore our faith in humanity, and the often elusive power of forgiveness.

For nine years, Brian Kuebler lived and breathed this story and has now punched through our televisions to deliver these characters and their true story in a compelling book you won't soon forget.

The Long Blink is a must read!

~ **Richard Sher** - Baltimore, Maryland
Longtime broadcast journalist | former Oprah talk show co-host

***

When Ed Slattery personally told me his tragic story years ago, I was moved beyond words. It's even more powerful and compelling in print. THE LONG BLINK saddens, informs and – ultimately – inspires us to take action against a growing danger on American roads.

~ **Congressman C. A. Dutch Ruppersberger**

***

What Ed Slattery endured could easily happen to any of us. This book captures an intensely personal and courageous journey after catastrophic loss. It challenges our basic understanding of grief, fatherhood and forgiveness. THE LONG BLINK is a fast, compelling read with an ending you will never see coming. Brian Kuebler's brilliantly-written true story is better than fiction. And, it is beautiful.

~ **Wayne Freedman**, 51 time Emmy award winning reporter | KGO-TV, ABC, San Francisco, author of *It Takes More Than Good Looks to Succeed at Television News Reporting*

BRIAN KUEBLER

THE
LONG
BLINK

**THE TRUE STORY
OF TRAUMA, FORGIVENESS,
AND ONE MAN'S FIGHT FOR SAFER ROADS**

Behler
PUBLICATIONS
USA

Behler Publications

The Long Blink
A Behler Publications Book

Library of Congress Cataloging-in-Publication Data
Names: Kuebler, Brian, author.
Title: The long blink / by Brian Kuebler.
Description: [Lake Jackson, Tex.] : Behler Publications, [2020] | Summary:
  "THE LONG BLINK is the true story about how a deadly crash involving one
  man's wife and children and a tired truck driver fuels his efforts to
  make America's roads safer for all -- and the explosive conclusion when
  he sets out to forgive the trucker"-- Provided by publisher.
Identifiers: LCCN 2019018647 (print) | ISBN 9781941887042 (pbk.) | ISBN
  194188704X (pbk.) | ISBN 9781941887059 (e-book)
Subjects: LCSH: Slattery, Ed. | Spouses of traffic accident victims--United
  States--Biography | Safety activists--United States--Biography | Truck
  accidents--United States. | Trucking--Accidents--United States. |
  Trucking--Accidents--Prevention--Government policy--United States. |
  Truck drivers--Health and hygiene--United States. | Truck
  driving--Safety measures. | Sleep deprivation. | Forgiveness.
Classification: LCC HE5614.2 .K85 A3 2020 (print) | LCC HE5614.2 .K85
  (ebook) | DDC 363.12/5092 [B]--dc23
LC record available at https://lccn.loc.gov/2019018647
LC ebook record available at https://lccn.loc.gov/2019980491

FIRST PRINTING

ISBN 13: 9781941887042
e-book ISBN 9781941887059

Published by Behler Publications, LLC, USA
www.behlerpublications.com
Manufactured in the United States of America

*For my wife Tiffany who absolutely
refused to let me stop writing.*

*And for my dog Shea,
who was curled up at my feet
for every last word.*

Table of Contents

INTRODUCTION

There are few stories in a journalist's career that challenge, exhilarate, or alter a reporter's worldview. Fewer still are the ones they remember, that are worth remembering. If you corner a journalist and ask them, they might very well regale you with a tale of how they helped change the world by getting a law created or signed in their local legislature, or maybe, for the true writers in some of us, the few times they were able to express the true human condition in a brilliant turn of phrase. There is honor in this profession and it is certainly achieved by such milestones, one story at a time.

I never set out to change the world. My journalism always had more of a modest goal, simply inform those who can. To me, that was nobler than claiming credit for any such law, or change in policy to protect whomever or whatever. So often our business rushes to take credit, warn, protect, and break. I simply told the stories I thought needed told; the hard, grimy, tough stories in a tough city. I was a crime reporter; my prism was blue and red flashing lights.

So when my boss at the time assigned me the story of Ed Slattery and his family, I hesitated. While I certainly knew it needed telling, I didn't see myself as the one to tell it. It was tragic. A trucker fell asleep at the wheel and crashed into the Slattery's car with a force so great, it would irrevocably alter the lives of everyone who felt the impact. It was simply a heartbreaking story, but not my lane. My news director thought differently and had the instinct and, ultimately, the faith to force me to think differently. I was assigned this story in autumn, 2010. Little did I know then how just one story would have impacted me about as much as I feel Ed Slattery's story has the power to impact you.

Ed Slattery is all of us, the everyman. Ordinary. It is the extraordinary that forced him to pivot in order to protect what was left of his family while using grief, the complex evasiveness of forgiveness and generosity, to fuel his fight to change an industry he blames. Crashes involving large commercial trucks kill thousands of people a year in this country. To be fair, not all crashes are the fault of truckers, but there are real issues of driver fatigue and the pressure created in a "pay by the mile" scheme many companies employ. Since the Slattery's crash in 2010, the fatalities from large trucks on American roadways have surged, and claim more than 4,000 lives each and every year.

The problem, as Ed Slattery and other advocates see it is not the truckers themselves, rather the complex combination of the amount of hours they are allowed to drive, rest times for those drivers and work shifts designed by some motor carriers. Slattery's story and others, like the crash that injured comedian Tracy Morgan, helped make the case to study federal regulations for motor carriers. Many experts say regulations, like the ones proposed in 2012, made our roads safer by increasing the rest drivers must get between certain shifts. Those changes were ultimately scrapped as the politics of regulation versus deregulation continue to ping pong between ruling parties on Capitol Hill. Still, at every turn, politicians meet Ed Slattery, a man who has made it his life's purpose to make our roads safer through common sense regulations.

Piecing your life back together after being shattered by such profound loss often looks like an incomplete puzzle with jaggedly shaped gaps in the picture. Ed Slattery channeled his grief and filled those spaces by weaving an incredible tapestry to honor his wife, Susan. From an advocate on Capitol Hill, to a cheerleader for his now-disabled son, and a philanthropist making his historic settlement earn good will rather than monetary interest, Slattery and his story saddens, inspires, and heals.

So yes, my goal as a journalist was not to change the world, rather inform those who can. But sometimes, just sometimes, the story is powerful enough to change the way a reporter sees the world.

PROLOGUE

When realities violently change, no matter the adjustments circumstance demands, you will always come to define life by the very last moment when it still was before what it now is; an almost visible emotional scar left by the turbulent shift of the tectonic plates that are conscience and sub-conscience.

Love. Loss.

Before. After.

With. Without her.

Chapter 1

There is perhaps no more unwelcome sound than a screaming alarm clock at 4:30 on a Monday morning, except for maybe the ring of a phone call that shatters the life you finally got right.

Ed Slattery rolled over the spot where his wife normally slept to slam the snooze button. Lying there in the fog that just about any commuter in the Baltimore/Washington area knows, he ran through the day ahead of him against the backs of his eyelids.

Ed was an economist with the United States Department of Agriculture. In short, he worked to help determine how many acres of organic crops were grown in the U.S. each year. There were databases to format, numbers to compare and, ultimately, a weathered pair of fifty-four- year-old eyes to cross. Not the ideal trade for an adult with attention deficit disorder, but solid work for a man who always found peace in the logic and predictability of numbers.

The numbers could wait though. To think of them at that moment was almost as unpleasant as the alarm that just sounded. The world hadn't woken up yet and there is always serenity in the calm before the giant gears of Baltimore and Washington start churning to do their part in making this country go. The few minutes before dawn were not meant for contemplating being a small cog in that wheel, not on this day; this was Ed's moment and he chose wisely to spend it thinking about his family.

His wife, Susan, and the couple's two children, Matthew, 12, and Peter, 16, were due home that evening and after ten days. Ed could no longer wait. Fresh off shoulder surgery, Ed didn't make it out to Susan's annual family reunion in Ohio. It was not choice, but circumstance, that had him packing up his wife and kids sending them for the getaway just outside Cleveland, Ohio.

Ten days was about nine days too long. While there are plenty of men who wear solitude well, it was not Ed's suit. A break from Susan and the boys was more like doing time, rather than having it all to himself. He always felt he did his best thinking and best living with his family. He felt incomplete when they were separated. It was an anxiety steeped in pain. Ed had been married before and was keenly aware of just how fragile a family life could be.

His children from his first marriage, now adults, were how and why he survived it. His marriage failed when his wife fell out of love as easily as she fell in. It was crushing and, for five years, Ed struggled with a cacophony of competing voices in his head: parent, homeowner, grad student, and ultimately, victim of unrequited love.

But the noise finally stopped in 1992. It was one of life's record-scratch moments when Ed found Susan Palmer. They were both working at Southwest Missouri State University, where Ed was a professor of Economics and Susan, a professor of Mathematics. Ed was immediately taken with her disarming charm and wry smile. Susan Palmer could do that to people. She had a warm look about her that invited others to drop their guards and engage in honest interaction. She had the kind of eyes that could rob you of your trepidation, which, in turn, gave her an intimate snapshot of your soul. She was smart, intimidatingly smart, but Susan never revealed it in an obtuse way. She was humble, caring, and kind.

After just two months, Ed proposed to Susan. Within two years, they had Peter, followed by Matthew. After time in Montgomery, Alabama, they moved to Baltimore, where Susan became a wildly popular Mathematics Professor at Stevenson University.

As a romantic realist, if there is such a thing, Ed knew life gives most of us one good pitch to hit for true love and complete happiness. But fate challenged Ed Slattery with this second fastball right down the middle, and he was waiting on it. Being in the middle innings of his life, Ed knew Susan, Peter, and Matthew were a near improbable game changer and he wanted them home, with him.

The thought of their return motivated Ed to make quick work of the day by launching out of bed toward the shower — but not before the mirror offered a glimpse back at a middle-aged man. His thinning, grey hair with matching beard was the perfect frame for his gentle face.

Ed studied himself. The wrinkles and crow's feet no longer a sullen reminder of age so much as they were the creases in an old road map that had taken him on his half century journey, confident in the wrong turns and detours life forced him to take toward the destination he now knew. A truth and comfortable certainty reflected warmly back at him through his own kind eyes.

No need to trim, looks great, Ed thought to himself as he paused to hear the crisp sound of his facial hair beneath his fingers. Ed spent the prior day cleaning, something he never did, but it served as much of a distraction for him as it would be a pleasant surprise for Susan. The family's three-bedroom lower-level apartment was still a bit cluttered, as usual, but it was clean and straight. Ed, while mostly driven by his heart, was also a pragmatic economist, and refused to settle into a home as the housing bubble was bursting wide open. He knew what many were just beginning to learn; purchasing a home in an affluent suburb was the wrong move at the absolute wrong time. An apartment close to one of the better schools in the area would do. Besides, his home was his two boys and Susan. No matter how clean it was, without his family, he couldn't help but feel like a stranger in a hotel.

House clean, man clean, he thought as he pulled back the shower curtain. A brisk five-minute shower was just about all that early in the morning would afford. Besides, for a woefully fashion-blind guy, getting dressed was going to require exponentially more thought. Susan always joked she was going to buy him Garanimals, children's clothing with animals that match tops with bottoms. Muted colors proved to be the adult version figuring Ed couldn't go wrong with khakis and navy blues. Choosing any particular combination was a win, bigger still if they were clean. It's the last decision he would have to make before stepping into the finely choreographed, mindless two-hour commute of light rail, commuter train, and metro that would take him from the Baltimore suburbs to downtown Washington, D.C.

More than enough people commute between the two cities every day, so it must be something a person can live with. But for Ed, it was the worst part of his day. He had only been doing it about two years, and in that time, he grew accustomed to seeing the same faces and having the same types of vapid conversations aimed at avoiding any tangible connection. That's not to say it's altogether shallow; there are groups that travel these roads, rails, and tunnels every day over the life of their careers and those men and women are part of a family built on routine and necessity, one hour at a time, five days a week. Not the perfect circumstance for building true friendships, but it can be done over a life's work. Ed was a newbie, just starting his white-collar sentence, not yet worthy of the kind of real interaction he craved with most everyone he met. That served his purpose on this day though, choosing to spend his energy meticulously planning the commute in order to shave just a few beats off the mundane.

It usually meant shaving just seconds or, if he was really lucky, minutes off the commute. But this day wasn't about saving time; it was about making time, making time for Susan and his two boys.

It was routine for Susan to call Ed making sure he got to work safely, even when she was on vacation. But by the time Ed reached his office, she hadn't called yet. Ed thought nothing of it and settled into his spreadsheets and numbers, columns and rows. The morning moved along and, when Ed still hadn't heard from Susan, he finally called her.

"We haven't left yet," Susan explained.

She sounded rushed to Ed, and he pictured his wife loading the car with the boys and their bags in her mother's driveway. One of seven children, goodbyes in Susan's family were always an event, and there was no such thing as a clean break. He understood that, obviously, but was altogether disappointed in the news. He had been back-timing his day to the nanosecond since 4:30 that morning, and it was now eleven o'clock and his family hadn't made any progress toward the moment he had been eager to experience for ten days. While his annoyance was perfectly understated in the tone of his response, it was never explicitly said. An inherently patient man, it was not his way.

"OK, honey. I love you, be careful," Ed said.

"I will, I love you, too," Susan responded before hanging up the phone.

The conversation was short and disappointing, making Ed more anxious. Having two young boys active in the Boy Scouts, Ed had been away from Susan for three weeks already that summer and had enough of the absence of his family and the woman he adored. Ed had been planning this reunion for the last several days, earlier telling Susan to be ready for N.O.R., his code for 'night of romance.' That was about as smooth as Ed Slattery would ever hope to be, especially for a married guy in his fifties, but as a man who finally figured out how to make life work for him, he didn't care. He missed his wife and his kids and felt deflated knowing they hadn't logged a mile toward that end.

"Focus, Ed!" he told himself. "Crunch these numbers and get home." Regardless of what Susan just said, he knew there were as many statistics as there were miles between them.

So, with a love for numbers only an accountant-turned-economist could have, Ed made those damn numerals dance, buckle, crunch, and read like a good novel, getting lost in the story line for a solid hour. It is not sexy work but it is logical, neat, and keeps chaos tied up in a basement somewhere so order rules, at least on a spreadsheet.

"Hello," Ed said as he picked up his cell phone without even looking at the number.

"Ed this is Human Resources at Goucher College," the voice said on the other end of the line.

"Ohhh...kay," he responded in a drawn out confused tone. Ed used to be an economics professor at the school in Baltimore County, but couldn't understand why they were calling him now.

"I really hate to call you under these circumstances, but I got a call from a Toledo hospital. It's your boys, Ed, they are in the hospital," she said.

"Well, that can't be, they are nowhere near Toledo," Ed told the woman as if she would even understand his confusion. His mind began to run through a series of scenarios in which this information would make sense. He couldn't find any.

"Well, they asked that you call. Let me give you the number," she said.

Ed jotted the number down on a random piece of paper and hung up thinking this must be a mistake. His fingers started to dial, but instinctively punched in Susan's number.

No answer, straight to voicemail. Ed pulled the phone away from his face and pressed 'End.' In the next few seconds, his mind rapidly flashed through some increasingly caustic thoughts: *surely Matthew or Peter would have picked up if Susan couldn't. But wait, why was the phone even off?* The intensity of this inner dialogue began punching holes in his gut, causing an uneasy emptiness, not in his heart, but in his very center, his soul. Refusing to let panic rush in, Ed dialed his mother-in-law.

"Ginger, it's Ed, have Susan and the boys left yet?"

"Yeah, they left about an hour ago."

"Well, I just got a call from my old employer telling me the boys are in a Toledo hospital. But you know what? Don't worry. They wouldn't be headed toward Toledo. Let me call this number the lady gave me and I will call you back," Ed said in a reassuring tone he knew lacked confidence.

He hung up and began dialing the number. As he punched in the Ohio area code everything began closing in, acutely unaware of the reality about to hit him while at the same time growing panicked with each number he pushed. He couldn't help but think if he hit 'Send,' he just might find fire near all this smoke.

"This is Ed Slattery, I was told to call this number, but I think this is a mistake," Ed meekly insisted.

His assertion was perhaps the last punch hope could throw at this rapidly impending reality.

"Mr. Slattery, this is Akron Children's Hospital," the nurse said in a tone suggesting she had been anticipating his call. *Akron makes sense*, he thought, *not Toledo*. But it would be the very last thing that would make sense to Ed Slattery for the rest of his God-given life.

"I'm sorry," the nurse continued, "your boys are here. They were in a very serious accident, and you need to get here as soon as possible."

It stunned him; her words knocked the wind out of him.

Ed gathered himself and, in the measured tone he always found most helpful in times of chaos, immediately fired off a short burst of questions parents are innately prepared to ask.

"Are they okay?"

"What happened?"

"How badly are they hurt?"

But the nurse couldn't provide any answers, not over the phone. She simply insisted it was best he get there as soon as possible.

Finally, Ed asked the one question a father works his whole life to avoid.

"Can you at least tell me if they are they alive?"

"Yes, Mr. Slattery, they are alive. I can't really go into details, but their injuries are serious."

"And my wife..." Ed's voice trailed as the remainder of his sentence got caught in his throat.

"I have no information about your wife, but let me give you some numbers of general hospitals in Akron."

The nurse rattled off numbers and, as Ed scribbled them down on yet another random piece of scrap paper, he couldn't help but think there was no order in these. There was no spreadsheet in the world that could make any sense of these numerals.

Chaos, he feared, broke free from that basement.

Ed started frantically dialing.

"Ginger, the boys are at Akron Children's. I need you to head there now, please."

"Oh my God, what happened?"

"Ginger, I don't know, and I haven't heard any news on Susan, but I need you to get to the boys."

Ed hung up his cell phone, picked up his office phone and dialed the first number the nurse gave him. It was Akron General Medical Center.

"Hi, I am trying to find my wife. Do you have a Susan Slattery?" he asked.

No record.

Hope, it seemed, finally landed a jab.

At an impasse, stuck somewhere between panic, horror, and ignorance Ed felt powerless. He walked across the hallway and told his boss his family was in some kind of accident, and he needed to leave.

As Ed turned around to walk back to his desk he started noticing some of his co-workers milling around his office as if sensing a volatile disturbance unfolding in slow motion. Staring at their concerned faces and still not knowing what his next move really needed to be, his desk phone rang snapping him back into a reality where indecision was never to be a luxury again.

"Is this Susan Slattery's husband, Ed Slattery?" the voice on the other end of the line asked.

"Yes," Ed offered abruptly.

"This is Doctor Roger Marcial from the Portage County Coroner's Office…"

Before the doctor could finish the statement he must have had the dubious distinction of delivering hundreds of times in his career, Ed interrupted with a disconnected anger that can only be expressed by a man finally accepting hope just got knocked on its ass.

"Oh," Ed blurted out.

His response halted the coroner on the other end of the line, and it was in that brief, deafening silence that Ed could almost hear the wave of trauma crashing onto the shore of his conscience as he finally put it all together.

"Well," Ed continued, "I guess she's dead?"

Chapter 2

"Well, Mr. Slattery, will you?" Dr. Marcial's voice punctured the brief-out-of-body experience Ed was having.

"I'm sorry, will I what?" Ed asked as if he didn't hear the coroner's question.

"Sir, do you want us to perform an autopsy?" the doctor repeated.

"Well, what for?" Ed exclaimed, "you just told me she got hit by a truck."

Ed wasn't the kind of man who led with emotion over reason, but his normal, measured approach was failing him. *An autopsy?* he thought. *I was just told my wife is dead and both my children are severely injured, and I'm supposed to be thinking post mortem? Post? I am still very much in the present!*

"Mr. Slattery, I know this is a tough question to hear, but you may want an autopsy done for legal purposes," the coroner said in a matter-of-fact, yet convincing tone.

Ed paused just long enough to entertain reason.

"Well okay," Ed decided, "I guess so."

Ed hung up his phone, still not quite grasping the enormity of that call, and studied the room. The milling about of concerned coworkers started to resemble a beautifully tragic ballet. Choreographed with looks of sorrow, legitimate hurt, and genuine concern, mere acquaintances were now watching him in an excruciatingly intimate moment.

Susan is dead?

Susan is dead.

Susan, my wife...killed in a crash with a truck?

No matter how many times he either asked or declared it in his head, that fact didn't feel right. It only served to continue to paralyze him. He was lost, jailed by those first heavy moments of grief that unleashed an unrelenting assault on his reality. Disbelief, though, still ruled Ed's mind.

This just can't be happening.

"Ed, you're booked," a voice said, breaking up the awfully loud, yet disconnected monologue Ed was having in his head.

"You are scheduled to fly into Akron. You leave from Reagan here in a bit and go through Charlotte," Cathy said.

Cathy was perhaps the closest friend Ed had in that office. The pair had worked together on many projects, and they worked together well. On this day, her project was Ed and, in that moment, she snapped him back into the reality he still had to face. Peter and Matthew were badly hurt. His boys needed him more than he needed to grieve. It was the right decision, the only decision; a fait accompli that rapidly rearranged his life and purpose.

"Okay," he responded, "but I have to call Susan's mother before we go."

As Ed said that, he realized that Susan's parents, Ginger and George, were still unwittingly on the other side of this grim reality. They still didn't know, they were still hoping and praying while driving to Akron.

Ed picked his cell phone off the desk and pushed the send button on the contact he last dialed. He didn't know what he wanted to say nor did he know what he was going to say. *It was best, to just say it,* Ed thought.

"Ginger. Susan is dead."

"Oh my God! My baby!" Ginger screamed.

In the background Ed heard Susan's father George ask what happened.

"Ginger, are you driving?" Ed asked. "Pull over!" he demanded.

There was rustling on the other end of the line and then Ed heard George pick up the phone and ask, "What happened?"

"Susan is dead, George," Ed said, "She was killed in the crash."

There was really no time to react to what was just said. Ginger and George were just told their youngest daughter was dead and their grandchildren lay in critical condition in Akron. Susan's parents were now presented with the same ugly predicament. They could be by the sides of their grandchildren within the hour. Ed was still twelve hours away. Peter and Matthew mattered more now. A daughter and wife gone, but this trauma was still unfolding in a children's hospital, and both boys needed all the family they had. Ginger and George got back on the road and, with the blurry and bloodshot eyes of parents who just discovered they had outlived their youngest daughter, they sped to be by their grandsons' bedsides.

In Washington, Ed prepared for hours of travel before he could lay eyes on his boys. In a panicked standstill, he forced himself to wrap around the idea that life as he knew it was simply over. It was a miserable and dramatic shift that kept him in an otherworldly state. The rest of his day would be a battle between being conscious and absent. Present, but not. Between the certainty and finality of Susan's death and the unknown of his sons' prognoses, he was riding the levels of the human condition like an elevator in a downtown high rise.

"What is this?" Ed asked as he felt his shirt pocket jostle with the weight of a man's hand.

"Ed, please. Just take it," a coworker insisted.

Two one hundred dollar bills were now folded up in Ed's breast pocket. Polite societal rules almost demanded he make a fuss at such an imposition of who was really just a pleasant acquaintance, but Ed was in no position to argue, nor could he. This was all theater, and Ed Slattery didn't quite understand his role.

Thankfully, Cathy did.

The two started to make their way from the office to Ronald Reagan National Airport, from the Farragut North stop along the red line to Gallery Place to transfer to the yellow.

The metro system in Washington, D.C. is simple, easy to navigate, clean and at some transfer points, just damn massive. Intimidating to some, but now on the platform waiting on the last leg that would take him straight to the airport, Ed felt like he could manage.

"Cathy, I'm fine. I got it from here."

"The hell you do, Ed," Cathy responded.

She must have said something else, but in Ed's mind she just trailed off into the seeming abyss that is the several story cavern of the Gallery Place transfer point.

Responding to her was pointless and Ed knew it. For a man that would normally go out of his way to avoid being an imposition to others, he was barely putting up a fight. He needed all his energy to tend to the battle of realities going on in his head.

Ed and Cathy were the only ones on that platform. It was one o'clock on Monday afternoon in August and the only audible sound was the gentle sigh riding the zephyr from deep within the tunnels.

Ed stared. He stared deep into the darkness of the southbound tunnel of the yellow line. His mind's eye began illustrating the emptiness, almost involuntarily. His brain, struggling between bouts of deep sorrow and panicked concern, produced a series of frenzied flash-frame memories.

The way Susan laughed…

Her chuckle would grow to the point of no return, an absolute loss of control. It was the kind of deep, hearty, tearful laughing fit that almost always ended with Susan exclaiming, "Oh my gosh," in her Midwestern accent. She became the glorious prisoner of whatever it was she found amusing. It was beautiful and comforting to watch.

The way Susan grounded him…

Ever the matriarch, if she looked at you from over the top of her glasses she expected your attention. If she began to point with her last three fingers while her pointer and thumb formed a circle, well then it was best to leave the room.

One after the other, these memories fired off between the synapses in Ed's mind as he remained standing on the platform in an otherwise catatonic state.

What the fuck is happening?

It was a refrain he would continue to repeat in lieu of any grasp of his past, present, or murky future.

Minutes later, the Huntington line roared out of the tunnel whistling past Ed and, within another fraction of a second, a violent wind gust slapped him in the face.

The light wasn't the end of his tunnel. It merely signified the beginning.

Ed made it to the airport, Cathy at his side. He was to board a USAir flight to Charlotte, then on to Akron. Ed flipped his phone open to see if he had a missed call while in the Metro. He noticed his battery was low, critically low, and his phone dying now was not an option.

Ed and Cathy walked through the terminal until they found a wireless store, one that would have a charger for his phone. The irony of purchasing a wire at the wireless store made Ed chuckle just a bit. In a day full of tragedy he could almost taste, light irony was the best attempt at cleansing his palate.

Cathy didn't stop there. She thought Ed needed a toothbrush and a comb. Who was he to argue?

With everything he needed packed into his breast pocket, Cathy sent Ed on his way, told him which gate, and pushed him toward security.

As Ed Slattery merged into the process of modern day air travel, he felt an ease in the anonymity of it all. He was able to find peace among perfect strangers. In a life now full of burden enough to crush most men, not having to talk about it was briefly freeing. No one in row 6 or seat C knew what just happened to Ed and he didn't have to tell them.

It was a peace shattered just hours later when his heart rate started to rise as the plane descended into Akron.

As Ed briskly walked out of the jet way and into the gate area he noticed just how barren it all was. Midnight in a regional airport is a quiet and lonely place. The terminal was dark. All the other flights had either arrived or left for the evening. As he took a minute to get his bearings he noticed the destination and departure time at his gate and others were already manually set for Tuesday, August 17th.

Technically it was the 17th, but Ed's life was stuck on August 16th.

Ed looked away from the dark gate area and noticed the main hallway in the terminal. Nothing was lit except the overhead lights and it looked like another dark tunnel.

He started to walk.

With no baggage he then started to jog.

Then Ed Slattery flat out sprinted down the hall of the main concourse of Akron Canton Airport. The overhead lights began to blend into one beam against the darkness of long closed Hudson News', Starbucks' and dim gates.

Ed finally reached the exit and then curbside to flag a cab.

"I need to get to Akron Children's Hospital as fast as possible," Ed told the cabbie breathless from his sprint, "My wife was killed in a truck crash and my two boys are in the hospital."

Ed couldn't help but think that was the first time he told anybody what happened.

The cab driver responded to Ed's tragic narrative by driving like a bat out of hell through the deserted streets of Akron, Ohio.

"Sir, I need to get there in a hurry, but I NEED to get there," Ed said from the back seat, "I am the only damned parent they have."

The cab pulled up in front of Akron Children's Hospital and stopped in the semi-circle driveway. Ed reached into his breast pocket and mindlessly dropped one of the hundred dollar bills onto the front seat and got out.

He stood there for just a beat, just a second. There was no sound in the humid summer night except for the idling cab behind him. The night was thick, soupy and still. As Ed Slattery looked up at the towering children's hospital in front of him, he couldn't help but realize he was at yet another strange doorstep of his life.

Chapter 3

The flash of the camera didn't so much as cause a flinch in Douglas Bouch's face. The forty-eight year-old's eyes remained wide, seemingly transfixed on an object that was right in front of him, yet couldn't quite see.

Still, not a muscle in his face twitched as the lens of some sure shot, dummy proof camera adjusted and clicked, taking his photo against a set of full-length wooden cabinets at the Ohio State Highway Patrol office in Berea, Ohio.

The picture came out blurred, but you could still plainly see a world of hurt and confusion behind Bouch's eyes.

As the state trooper raised the camera again to take a better photo of who would be referred to in the crash report as Unit #01, his face remained stoic, as if frozen in a moment that was jailing his very soul.

The time was 1:22 p.m. on August 16, 2010, almost two hours after the crash, but Bouch seemed stuck in the seconds before he struck Susan Slattery's Ford Focus while heading east on the Interstate 80, the Ohio Turnpike.

In 1998 Bouch became a driver for Estes Express Lines, a company he said was solid and well-regarded in the industry. His pay was as steady as the work, and it helped him build a life and raise a family in Greenville, Pennsylvania, a small town half way from Cleveland to Pittsburgh.

On August 16, 2010, Douglas started his day at about 1:30 in the morning. It was his first night back, the start of his week. Not a true midnight shift, but close enough as the alarm sounded early that morning after a long Sunday tending to parts of his farm outside of Greenville.

By 2:30 Bouch had made the 17-mile drive south to the small town of West Middlesex, Pennsylvania to pick up his load for the day. By 3:00 a.m., he was headed west out of Pennsylvania to the beginning of the Ohio Turnpike where he increased his load to three trailers.

Triples, as they are called in the industry, are only legal in certain states, and Ohio is one of them. In this current assignment for Estes, Doug was hauling what the industry calls LTL or less than truck load. LTL are trailers filled with just about anything the American consumer would ever buy; from computers, to pens to the shower curtain you can pick up at Target.

At mile marker 209, along the Ohio Turnpike, Doug would add the third trailer, maximizing the load through a state that allowed this kind of haul. From the east end of Ohio to Fremont, Indiana on the west end and then back again, Doug was paid 53¢ a mile. That day, he would travel just more than 500 miles for a total of $271.36.

It was a route Bouch said he'd run many times before. He said he never really liked driving triples; they were tougher to haul, harder to maneuver, and required another level of caution to control. That last trailer, or pup, is nicknamed a wiggle wagon because, as some drivers will tell you, they are the least responsive and can wiggle above certain speeds. Sometimes, Doug said, he would go well below the speed limit just to maintain more control. It also took much longer to brake.

Speed could cause a problem, so could weather; Bouch understood driving a triple was a world of difference from the twenty-two years he spent driving just two trailers. What may be a two-foot adjustment up front can mean one hundred feet in the back. Nothing is instant in a triple he said.

But still, living near the Ohio state line, Estes wanted Bouch to haul the legal truck configuration across the state, drop it, pick up another, and haul it back. It was a route he had done hundreds of times, so much so he knew the miles without the markers, including the one that would come to mark the decimation of two families.

"Mr. Bouch, did you understand your rights as I read them?" Sergeant J.R. Miller of the Ohio State Highway Patrol asked.

It was the first question Doug Bouch was asked in the roadside interview, a necessary and timely investigative tactic meant to preserve accurate memory of an incident. Time is the enemy in crash investigations and, while there would be plenty of it for formal processing later in the afternoon at the police station, first impressions and instant recall from those directly involved were crucial.

"Yes, sir," Bouch responded as he leaned up against the jersey wall still physically and emotionally shaken from what just happened.

"Can you tell me what happened in the crash?" the sergeant asked.

"I was coming down the hill and I guess I dozed off. When I opened my eyes I saw brake lights, people coming to a stop. I could not stop. I could not veer. I looked for an out, but there was nowhere I could go. I slammed on my brakes. I stood on them as hard as I could."

"Were you injured?"

"Not that I am aware of, but I'm pretty shook up. Just before the impact I tensed up. I pushed against the steering wheel and braced myself."

The sergeant scribbled notes and briefly moved onto a few procedural questions about seatbelt, road conditions, and if Bouch recalled what lane he was in.

He answered all of them correctly according to the police record, but then the officer started down a line of questioning to get at exactly what happened at mile marker 190.5.

"Do you remember the first vehicle you struck?"

"No," Bouch responded. "I'm guessing, but I believe it was a red one."

He got that question right, too. Beyond where the two men were standing was indeed a red mangled mess that was a Ford Focus. The color of that car was just about the only thing recognizable, the rest of it at that moment was a twisted ball of steel, plastic, and glass. Bouch didn't look in that direction as a bevy of medical personnel and fellow crash victims were tending to the traumatic aftermath.

"You said you dozed off," the sergeant said. "Can you elaborate?"

"I guess I dozed off. When I opened my eyes I saw brake lights."

"How much sleep did you have in the last twenty-four hours?"

"Probably about three hours and twenty minutes," Bouch responded, "I woke up Sunday at 9:30 a.m. I stayed awake to about 10 p.m. and went to sleep. I slept until about 1:20 a.m. My alarm was set for 1:20 a.m. I have been awake from 1:20 a.m. until now."

He had been awake 11 hours, fueled only on just a shade more than three hours sleep.

"Is that normal for you?" the officer asked.

"This is my first day of the week, and I have trouble sleeping the first day. I forced myself to sleep from 10:00 p.m. to 1:00 a.m."

Bouch then walked the sergeant through his shift including a brief 10-minute stop at the travel plaza at mile marker 140.

"Did you stop anywhere else?"

"No."

"Are you taking any medication?"

"Yes. Fluoxetine, 80mg. This is for Fibromyalgia. I also take Mobic, 15 or 25mg. This is also for Fibromyalgia. I take it in the afternoon before I go to bed."

"Did you take this medication on Sunday?"

"Yes."

The questions persisted along that line; illegal drugs, alcohol, over the counter medication? Bouch answered no to all of it. It had been since the 4th of July that he had a drink and his toxicology results would confirm no trace of any alcohol or illegal drugs.

The sergeant then circled back again to a line of questioning that would remain key to the smoldering pile of twisted and charred steel and plastic strewn across a now-closed Ohio Turnpike just yards away, "Do you know what milepost you're at?" the officer asked.

"Around 190," Bouch responded, "I know the route."

"You said you opened your eyes and you saw brake lights. Why was traffic stopping?" Sergeant Miller probed.

"I don't know. I assume construction. There were signs about a mile back about the two lanes closed ahead."

"Can you estimate how long you dozed off?"

"No."

"How do you feel now?"

"Weirded out," Bouch told the officer.

"Has anything like this happened to you before?"

"I have had some scares in the past. I learned from the past, and now I pull over and rest."

It was about all the officer had for Douglas Bouch on the scene of the accident.

Seven more witnesses were interviewed on that scene, all of them corroborating what police would eventually write up in their report.

Douglas Bouch fell asleep at the wheel while hauling his triple tractor-trailer through Ohio. He dozed off as he approached construction that was forcing motorists to merge from three lanes down to just the far left lane.

As drivers were slowing to merge, maybe 15 to 20 miles per hour many of them would recall, it happened.

The witnesses were from all over, the kind of cross section of America one would expect to find on a Midwestern turnpike. All of them could remember hearing what happened before looking up and seeing it.

Jennifer Eades of Michigan described that very sequence of events to an officer, as did Trevor Baumann of Fairview Park, Ohio, who could remember seeing the Estes tractor-trailer "come plowing through the traffic," hitting another semi that was to his right.

In that semi was Jonathan Weidman of Rothbury, Michigan. He drove for Covenant Transport and told the police that it all came out of nowhere, and he remembered looking up to see his back trailer peeling toward him. "All of my belongings were raining down on me from the truck's compartments," he said in his scene interview. "The Estes truck was scraping all the way down the left side of my truck and bashing anything in front of it out of the way." Wiedman remembered watching Bouch's truck burst into flames as it hit the jersey wall and smashed cars everywhere.

Wiedman told the trooper who interviewed him that once it all stopped, "I looked in my right mirror and saw a red car under the right side of the back of my trailer. I went to the car to see if anyone was in it. I saw people in it, but they weren't moving."

He would call 911.

Dispatchers were getting many calls from mile marker 190.5 on the Ohio Turnpike, including one from Trevor Baumann, who at this point was approaching what was left of a red Ford Focus under the back of Wiedman's trailer.

"I could see the mother breathing slowly," Baumann would tell Lieutenant William Weirtz in his interview. "The boy in the passenger seat was passed out with blood running from his nose. A doctor arrived on the scene and broke out a window and said the boy was dying."

Baumann said the doctor kept working on the younger boy in the front seat as he and a highway worker kept the other boy in the back seat speaking until the paramedics arrived.

Like a puzzle, all of the witness statements, including that of Bouch himself, pieced together the picture of what happened.

It was that picture that undoubtedly paralyzed Doug Bouch's mind, his blank stare impervious to the bright flash of the camera back at police headquarters.

While certainly no one knew if it was criminal, based on his roadside interview, police knew Bouch was at least culpable. Troopers spent the last few hours preserving what they could for the crash report and subsequent investigation.

The trooper, making sure to correct his original blurred picture of the Estes driver, took several more. Even as the camera angle changed from a head shot to a full length photo, Douglas Bouch's expression in each of the four images remained exactly the same; a middle aged American man wearing a blue uniform shirt, jeans, boots, and a world of hurt, confusion, and fear.

The time was 1:23 in the afternoon of August 16, 2010.

Time was no longer an enemy of the investigation; it was now becoming a formidable force, as state investigators would begin developing the criminal case against Doug Bouch.

Chapter 4

Ed Slattery stood in front of Akron Children's Hospital in the still of the late Ohio night. He stared at the entrance not knowing what to expect. Life had just violently shuffled the deck on him once again. On the other side of those doors was his life rearranged, not at all as he had left it. Not for his boys, and certainly not for his wife.

Ed walked toward the entrance of the hospital. The double doors shot open with urgency as a burst of cold air hit him in the face. It was dark in the lobby, but there was a receptionist off to the right. Ed barely made eye contact with the woman before he started reading her eyes, and she his.

"My name is Ed Slattery," he said breathless from the anxiety of what awaited him upstairs.

Without even looking at a chart or a computer the woman interrupted him as if she was expecting him and pointed him to the elevator and simply said, "Fourth Floor."

Ed moved toward the bank of elevators and pushed the button. One of the cars was there waiting. He pushed '4' and watched out the glass enclosure as he rose through the lobby of the building in a soft floating motion. The gentle, gliding ride was quickly interrupted with a ding.

The doors parted, sliding open onto a dark hallway. Looking left, he could see some light coming from the end of the hall, but absolutely no signs of anyone or any thing.

"Is anybody here?" Ed yelled. "I need help, is anybody here?"

A figure appeared at the end of the hallway near the light. Ed yelled again, "I am Ed Slattery, you have my boys!"

Ed hurried toward to the pediatric nurse who led him down yet another dark hallway. Behind another set of doors, Ed stepped into an area that looked like it specialized in taming chaos. It was well lit, spacious, and swimming in medical machines and charts that, in these off hours, were quietly set to the side, but ready for action at a moment's notice. The only distinct sound was the humming and beeping of medical equipment serving as the soundtrack to the concerned and prayerful.

Ed was in the Pediatric Intensive Care Unit. The nurse directed him to the waiting room at first. There, he saw all of his in-laws, all of them sitting in chairs, their faces wearing the emotional trauma of the past twelve hours.

Ed looked at the room. Before anyone could notice him, he turned to the nurse and said, "No. Take me to the boys. Where are my boys?"

The nurse took Ed around the corner and to a room closed off by a pair of sliding glass doors. Just outside were two nurses tethered to computers monitoring all those machines and the litany of sounds they were making.

Ed pulled the door open and walked in to see his twelve-year-old boy in a very grown up contraption. The image halted him. Ed had been racing across the country all day to get to this moment, not knowing what he would see, and now, not quite understanding what he saw. There were hoses or tubes going in and coming out of almost every hole or accessible vein. Matthew's right eye was puffy and a deep purple, a machine was doing the breathing for him, and his head was covered in white bandages.

"He looks so little," Ed whispered to himself, as if the trauma was two sizes too big on his little boy. But as he studied Matthew between the tubes and bandages, focusing on just the small parts of his child he could plainly see, Ed didn't recognize him. Matthew's innocence was wrapped up in those bandages, too. His infectious laugh, which he shared with his mother, was silenced. Matthew was a boisterous, active kid...but that, too, seemed covered up by the medical equipment keeping him alive. All the more complicated was the fact that Ed could do nothing to fix his baby boy. He grew angry at what happened and, irrationally, angry with himself. But as the ventilator cycled to the next mechanical, robotic breath, practically jumping his pre-teen's chest, Ed could not help but repeat one thought to himself over, and over, and over, and over again.

He is alive.

"Mr. Slattery," Ed heard the nurse say, interrupting his inner dialogue.

Colette was the trauma nurse assigned to both Matthew and Peter. She would be Ed's point of contact for anything medical. Ed looked up to catch her gaze; his soft, yet exhausted eyes said what he didn't have the energy to say.

"Mr. Slattery," she repeated with a gentle, warm but concerning smile, "I am going to explain what it is you're looking at."

Colette looked back down at the chart and started to drown Ed in words that he didn't fully understand.

"Matthew was flown to us from the scene of the accident near Streetsboro, Ohio on Interstate 80," Colette said. "He was unstable and unresponsive. Our team went to work right away to give him fluids and blood to raise his blood pressure and identify his visible injuries. His biggest physical injury is a laceration from his left ear to the back of his head, with a very obvious fracture to his skull."

Colette was trying to be as gentle and delicate as possible, telling Ed what he needed to know, but not everything doctors did know.

Matthew's laceration, as she put it, was what gave trauma doctors an unobstructed view of a depressed skull fracture. Because of the large cut in Matthew's head, it was easy for doctors to see partially collapsed skull and brain matter.

She could sense Ed pulling back as he struggled to comprehend these very real injuries to his innocent boy. Colette chose a lighter touch as she continued, focusing more broadly on Matthew's condition.

"Once we got him more stable, we were able to take Matthew to a CT scan, so we could get a really good look at all his injuries. Basically, all of Matthew's injuries are in his head. His skull is fractured in multiple places, including his face, but more urgently, he had a significant amount of bleeding in and around his brain."

Colette looked up from her chart to gauge how Ed was receiving all this medical jargon, and found him staring at Matthew. He didn't seem to notice her pause, so she took that as the opportunity to continue.

"So the bleeding was putting a fair amount of pressure on Matthew's brain, and we had to move pretty quickly to the operating room. There, our surgeons had to take away parts of the skull to treat the bleeding and relieve the pressure."

Normally, when doctors perform this procedure they save the fragment of skull they remove to then replace it later. It wasn't an option for Matthew. The impact of the crash damaged his skull so badly, he would need a prosthetic when, or if, he healed.

Colette knew there was no real way to gently deliver the description of that procedure, so she tactfully left out how surgeons peeled away the parts of Matthew's skull broken from the impact to stop the bleeding.

She would also leave out the part where doctors had to insert what is essentially a tire pressure gauge for the brain by drilling yet another hole in Matthew's head.

For now, on that first night as Ed continued to stare at his twelve- year-old child, he'd been told enough. Colette stopped talking. The only sound was the robotic rhythm of the ventilator and the various beeps of different monitors.

It was a good minute before Ed, without turning away from Matthew, asked the question he had been rehearsing in his mind for the past twelve hours.

"Is he gonna live?"

Colette's pause was palpable. She was very measured in her response, so to be realistic, but without creating false hope, she said softly, "The next twenty-four hours are crucial, Ed." Despite her efforts, Ed started to contemplate the cold uncertainly of that response.

"Where's Peter?" he asked.

Colette brought Ed to the sixth floor of the hospital to see his older son.

He saw Peter sitting more upright, with far fewer tubes and bandages.

Peter had suffered a broken pelvis, a bruised face, and a broken eye socket. All considered, he faired pretty well compared to Matthew and Susan.

"All bones, right?" Ed turned back to Colette and asked, "No brains."

"Yes, Ed, we have Peter pretty well sedated because he is in a lot of pain. But his injuries are not as complicated."

Peter would require a host of surgeries of his own, but he would survive. Ed and the doctors knew that.

What Ed didn't know was, what to do, or where to be. He was the only parent his boys had, and he didn't want either one of them to wake up and not see him.

Thus began a night where Ed Slattery would march back and forth between the fourth and sixth floors.

From Matthew's room, he would briskly walk past the nurses' station and through the double doors. On the right was the waiting room, and then just past that were two elevators.

Push the UP button, wait, doors open, get in, push '6'.

It was always a short ride, but the solitude in that elevator allowed Ed to lean against the back railing and take a deep breath between witnessing the atrocities afflicted on either of his two boys.

"What the fuck," Ed began asking himself under his breath. But each and every time, his disbelief and confusion were met with the elevator doors opening up onto his very real tragedy: There's a fish tank to the right, jog straight to Peter's room, zigzag around another nurses' station to the last door on the right. Spend ten minutes, watch Peter breathe, get anxious, jog back down the hallway past the nurses' station and the fish tank, push the button, elevator doors open immediately, it was usually still there, waiting. "What the fuck," Ed would mumble on the ride down. It became his mantra of the evening, "What the fuck. Susan, what am I going to do?"

Ed stopped muttering and reminded himself quietly that his wife was dead. The car stopped, leveled off and the doors opened onto the fourth floor. Ed took a second and stared out onto the floor before he declared to himself he was not to mourn his wife at that moment, not for himself and, most importantly, not for his critically injured children.

Ed pushed himself off the back rail of the elevator, where his hands were behind his back, cushioning his backside. He took the next step in what was going to be a long journey of roaming the halls and trying, quite literally, to be in two places at one time. If either of his two sons were to open their eyes again, the first thing he wanted and needed them to see was his face.

Ed Slattery never did sleep that first night.

His mind was in a constant state of turmoil. There would be no rest until his body demanded it. Staring at Matthew, the rhythm of the machine keeping him alive lulled him into a brief micro sleep...his body shutting down what his brain didn't need, until he was nudged awake by the day shift nurse.

"Mr. Slattery," she whispered, "your family is back."

Ed had no concept of time other than the sun being back up again. He must have passed out by Matthew's bedside. He stood up, removed his glasses and pinched his eyes before walking out of Matthew's room and into the PICU waiting area.

Ed saw Susan's mother, father, and sisters; Matthew and Peter's cousins. The family was clearly just as restless, exhausted, and emotionally confused as he.

"I am going to need two of you at all times," he declared.

Ed realized during the time it took roaming the halls between rooms making sure neither of his boys was without their sole parent, both of them were.

"When I'm with one, I'm not with the other, and when I'm in between, I'm not with either."

That simply could not happen. It would not happen. From that point forward, one member of the family was with Peter and one with Matthew, allowing Ed the travel time to march from one to the other.

That first morning became afternoon, and as more family arrived, including his daughter Kelli from Baltimore, Ed began to settle into a life where he was at the mercy of the two sets of machines keeping his boys alive.

But unbeknownst to Ed, it was one of those instruments, the one attached to Matthew's forehead that began signaling an alarming number, bringing the neurosurgeon into the room.

"Mr. Slattery, my name is Roger Hudgins, I am Matthew's neurosurgeon," he said in that matter-of-fact way some doctors talk to lay people. Not offensive by any means, just curt and to the point because, as he was about to tell Ed, there wasn't much time to chit chat.

He explained how Matthew's intracranial pressure was incredibly high, it was registering in the mid 30's, when it should have been half that number. The newest CT scan told the team there was a significant amount of pressure on Matthew's brain.

Ed remained silent but attentive as the doctor continued.

"Here is what we want to do, I want to take Matthew back to the OR, remove a piece of his skull, and relieve the pressure."

The procedure was exactly as it sounded but the surgeon explained how he felt if his team was to continue to do everything for Matthew, then it was the right move. He explained to Ed that he couldn't guarantee it was going improve his son's outcome or make him better. The enemy was swelling and pressure and it needed to be relieved. There were other options, though.

"We can wait it out or continue certain drugs, but you need to know that every moment his brain is under this kind of pressure, it could be damaging his recovery if there is to be one," Dr. Hudgins said.

Ed looked the surgeon in the eye and said, "Do what you have to do."

Doctor Hudgins left the room to notify the OR.

Ed was never much of a praying man and didn't at that moment. He simply slid back in his chair without taking his eyes off Matthew and watched a team of people in scrubs invade the room and take his son away to the OR.

Suddenly Ed was in an empty room accompanied only by anxiety, a sustained and high level of emotional trauma, and a near constant state of urgency. The only physical reaction to it all was to put his head between his legs and sob the way an adult rarely ever does, forcing Ed to submit to heavy, raw emotion. Losing complete control of muscles or dignity, his face contorted and his voice wailed.

"Mr. Slattery," a soft voice said from behind him. "I don't mean to bother you, but I wanted to offer you some of our services to you and your family during your sons' stay here at the hospital."

Ed turned to see a social worker assigned to his case. Wiping away tears and gaining control of himself, he briefly entertained the distraction. The woman tried to discuss a place to stay for his family at the Ronald McDonald House, facilities to use while spending overnights in the hospital, any medications Ed himself was on that could be transferred, and so on.

The logistics were catching up with the trauma, but Ed couldn't focus on them. He interrupted the woman, "Ma'am. Could you please get a message to the surgeon?" he asked without expecting the niceties of an answer right away. "If the doctor thinks my son is going to die on the operating table, I want to be in there holding him as he passes. If you need to tape his skull up, fine, just let me see him."

Matthew didn't die on that table, although no one knew if he was going to survive.

The craniectomy only worked temporarily. The pressure in Matthew's skull began to increase yet again, but this time cutting into his skull was no longer an option. Another CT scan revealed a buildup of fluid, and doctors chose to insert a drain.

It went on that way for a week. Back and forth, walking a tightrope between life and death. There was literally nothing else the doctors could do for Matthew but wait, hope, and pray.

A couple of floors above, Peter was recovering. He went through the first of several surgeries and the sixteen year-old was just beginning his own long and complicated journey. Matthew, however, continued to struggle. There was never an easy day.

It had been a week after the crash and still no one knew if the twelve year-old was going to survive and, if he did, certainly no one knew what quality of life he was going to have.

Ed never left the hospital, not even for fresh air. His brother-in-law bought him new clothes. He showered in bathrooms meant for the parents and ate hospital food. All the while his family came and went every day begging him to do the same and take a break. His response was always, "I am not leaving my boys."

And he didn't, until he had to.

Chapter 5

Susan was dead.

While Ed still hadn't grasped the emotional realities of that, he was reminded of the cold fact when he was brought the release from the Coroner's Office. The autopsy he agreed to just a couple of days before ruled her cause of death multiple blunt force trauma to the head, neck, and torso.

The words read very academic to him. He knew what they meant, but couldn't rightly define how they were responsible for his wife being gone. But as he continued to read the document, he saw a receipt listing the belongings taken off Susan's body. Ed slowly read through the items, thinking how this was all just a morbid formality, the kind of thing no one ever really thinks they'll ever have to do. Her shirt was first on the list followed by the socks she was wearing, her trousers, and underpants. Then Ed noticed the last entry on the form. "Shoes." Except he saw that someone had struck through the last 's' on the pre-typed word. He paused at the absurdity of it. *Only one shoe? Where the hell was her other shoe?*

It was the last thought Ed had before signing the release outside of Matthew's hospital room. When it came to Susan, he found it more helpful to focus on the logical to stave off the emotional. In some weird way the whole process surrounding her death almost seemed like a footnote or a chore. Certainly Ed didn't actually feel that way but as his mind and body was forced to deal with so many traumas, burying Susan's death deep into his subconscious was a necessary defense mechanism.

Ed couldn't emotionally deal with the death of his one true love, not yet. He was not sure he had the mental faculties to survive such a stark reality, and he knew Susan would have insisted he spend the time and energy on their boys. It was a comfortable thought. It made sense and gave Ed an excuse to look away from the even deeper end of this tragic abyss.

Focus on the boys. It is what Susan would most definitely want and what Ed needed, until his phone rang. On the other end was a funeral director asking questions that threatened to pull back the curtain on this self-imposed charade of a coping mechanism he constructed in his mind.

"Do you want to have a wake? Where does Susan want to be buried? Have you discussed caskets?" The inquiries just kept coming, like a grim version of twenty questions. Still, they were details that needed attention.

"Well, I know Susan wants to be cremated, sir. Beyond that, I'm not sure I know how to direct you any further."

Ed mentally could not add any more to that conversation and physically could not take on any more responsibility. Utterly overwhelmed, he told the funeral director that Susan's parents would handle the details of the wake.

The Palmers decided on an Akron funeral home where Susan was viewed during a small ceremony. The idea of it seemed preposterous to Ed. Akron didn't care about Susan Palmer Slattery. What viewing would she have? Her life was back in Baltimore, her past just outside Cleveland. It felt to Ed he was burying his wife somewhere in between like the settlers did, on the side of a trail during the migration west. There was no dignity in it, and Ed didn't want to give it any.

It is why when the day came to leave the hospital for the very first time since the crash, Ed felt forced. So much happened in seven days and so much more was still ahead for both his sons. Peter had just had another surgery, this time on his hip. Ed didn't want to leave Peter and Matthew. Still, knowing it meant something to Susan's parents and that it was simply the right thing to do, Ed begrudgingly left his boys and traveled across Akron to physically say goodbye to a woman who still very much mentally filled his present being.

Ed's oldest daughter Kelli helped her father, driving him to the funeral home. Ed needed the support. Being in a car for the first time since he arrived at Akron Children's Hospital, Ed was struck by views of a world that had obviously kept moving. With his head resting against the passenger side window, he scanned the people and cars and homes passing by. It felt otherworldly to him. Indefinitely suspended by trauma, in his mind it was still August 16th, but for these people he saw, they were living in a present that, to him, should still be the future.

As he pulled up to the funeral home, Ed couldn't help but think it was rundown. His observation was only confirmed as he walked up to and into the old house. The floors creaked and the décor reeked of manufactured grief; a noxious combination of old velvet upholstered furniture and embalming fluid.

At the door was the funeral director who greeted him and showed him to the room where his Susan was. The funeral director stopped at the back of the room and allowed Ed to walk in by himself. He walked slowly to the front where Susan's coffin was nestled in a small alcove.

As Ed approached, he couldn't help but think the last time he physically saw her was weeks ago when he sent her and the boys off to Ohio. It felt like a lifetime between then and this moment.

Ed made it to the side of the casket, looked directly at Susan's face...and wept.

"Oh, sweetie. I am so sorry," Ed cried, pulling off his glasses and pinching the corners of his weary eyes against the bridge of his nose.

He peered down at his wife's body, blurred through his tears. As his eyes focused on Susan, all Ed could feel was immense sorrow. Sorry he wasn't there when it happened. Sorry she would never see Matthew become a teenager or Peter grow into a young man. Ed hated that he couldn't prevent what happened even though there was nothing he could have done. The what-ifs, too, were a crushing burden. What if he put his family in a bigger car or...goddammit...what if Susan had left when she was supposed to? Why the hell was she not on the road when he called that morning. If she had, maybe she would have been further down the road when that trucker fell asleep. Maybe, just maybe...

The grief was heavy. Ed could feel it weighing on his soul, and then his physical being. He braced against the casket and composed himself. As the first wave of emotion receded, he allowed himself to continue studying Susan.

"You look hideous, honey," he said out loud as if Susan could hear him.

It was as if he was looking at a stranger. The woman in that rented coffin was not Susan. She was not wearing her glasses, the teal button down blouse was not hers and the caked on make-up simply made her look unrecognizable. Susan never wore make-up.

Ed spent another minute looking at the caricature of how the mortician viewed his wife before walking off to a bench beneath a bay window to sit down. Ed looked around the quiet room and then back at the body he was to help pass off as his wife.

"This is ridiculous," he muttered.

There was nothing in that casket that resembled his wife and nothing about the viewing that could justify him not being at the hospital with his boys. He may not have been ready to mourn Susan for a myriad of reasons, and felt certain he wasn't going to do it at that moment, not in that way.

Ed stood back up and walked out to the car. He opened the car door and sat in the passenger seat, Kelli was at the wheel.

"Let's go back to the hospital," Ed said.

"That body in there is not my wife, and she would want me back with the boys. If either of them wake up, I need to be the first thing they see."

Without saying a word, Kelli put the car in gear and returned his father to the building he would not leave again for another two weeks.

Ed Slattery was tethered to Akron's Children's Hospital because in it was all he had left. As the days continued to pass, while Matthew's prognosis improved minimally at best, Peter began to make some significant strides and get stronger.

Peter's hip surgery kept him on a lot of pain medications but his physical injuries were healing at a hopeful rate. Enough so that one night, well after visiting hours, Ed invited him to make the trip to the fourth floor to see his brother for the first time since the crash.

Peter agreed.

Ed wheeled his son down that hallway, past the nurses' station, into the elevator, and pushed the button for the fourth floor.

Father and son went down the next hallway through the double doors and into Matthew's room.

Ed stopped the chair and stood behind him while Peter remained silent and gazed at his younger brother. The two stayed like that for a solid five minutes, not one word was spoken until Peter finally looked up at his father and nodded.

Ed backed the wheel chair out of Matthew's room, through the double doors and to the elevator that was still there waiting.

The doors opened on the sixth floor, and it was just past the fish tank when Peter finally lost it. The sixteen year-old started crying uncontrollably.

Ed let him have a minute, let him sob as he leaned down to embrace his son. It went on that way for a few minutes before Peter stopped crying. Ed released him from his fatherly hug, kneeled down and told Peter what he felt he needed to know but wasn't quite sure he knew.

"Peter, Mommy died in the crash."

Ed braced for another long and emotional hold, but Peter simply looked up at his father with his bloodshot eyes.

"I know."

Ed wondered how long his teenager was struggling with that reality by himself. He felt guilty for not helping share that burden sooner. His son was drifting in and out of consciousness from drug-induced hazes, only to be repeatedly hit with that emotional anvil of a reality, and it seemed magnified in his son's tears as he gazed upon his father. It was a world of hurt Ed wanted so badly to lift off his boy, and perhaps himself.

Ed finished wheeling Peter to the last room on the right. He put his injured son to bed, kissed him on the forehead, and slipped out of his room quietly as he fell fast asleep.

"Hello?" Ed said as he fumbled to flip open his ringing cellphone in the quiet hallway.

"Hi, I'm looking for a Peter Slattery."

"Um, this is his father," Ed responded in a confused tone, "How…what…who is this?"

"Well, I am a driver. I've been driving trucks for a while tonight and needed a break, so I pulled over on the side of the road and walked a lap or two around my rig to wake myself up," the man said. "Anyway, I found this wallet here on the shoulder, and it has a Peter Slattery's information in it, so I figured I would call."

There is happenstance and kismet…for the religious there is even divine intervention to explain moments like this, but Ed was dumbfounded by this confluence of events. Given his last few weeks, it struck him that he should have been more stunned at the absurd irony of it all, if not for being all out of that particular emotion.

He struggled to find the words to respond.

"Um, well, um…that is my son's wallet. Last week he, my youngest son, and wife were in a bad wreck. My wife died and both my boys are in the hospital. I mean, I guess you pulled over in that same spot if that is where you found my boy's wallet."

The driver remained silent on the other end. Ed may not have been able to see the rich irony, but the driver seemed paralyzed by it.

Ed continued, "Sir, thank you for being alert enough to stop and get some air before continuing on your route."

Ed wouldn't believe it himself if he hadn't just taken the call. It was one of so many amazing moments along this journey he was in as a father and a widower. But as powerful, ironic, or symbolic as it was, it still paled in comparison to day-to-day, and sometimes hour-to-hour progress of his two boys. Slow but finally, real and promising progress Ed wanted to share with friends and family back home in Baltimore in an on-line journal he committed to updating, sometimes several times a day.

Aug 23, 2010
Dear friends and family,

We had a big pow-wow with about a dozen doctors and the consensus is that Matthew will make it through this. There are no guarantees, but I am more hopeful today than I have been in days. He has a long way to go but, rest assured, we whisper in his ear and give him kisses all the time. I have read him some of the cards you all sent but don't want to overwhelm his very sore little brain all at once. I'll keep reading some to him every day.

August 25, 2010
Dear family and friends,

Matthew is off of the coma-inducing medication and coughs when they suction his lungs. It will be several days before those meds are out of his system and then we hope he'll open his eyes. If all goes well, he'll have a body scan, surgery to fix his jaw, and have a trach put in on Friday. If that all goes well, he may be able to be transported to Baltimore in another week or so after that.

Sep 3, 2010
Dear family and friends,

Matthew underwent six hours of surgery today. They put in a trach, a feeding tube in his stomach, and fixed his jaw. The jaw took a long time, as they had to be careful about nerves and work around braces. He lost one adult tooth in the procedure, but it was badly damaged and right on the fracture line.

This feels like a step backwards to me but I know it's not really. It's just that we were making some progress and now he's knocked out again. He does look better without all of those tubes coming out of his mouth and nose. I can see my little boy again. He has a cool scar on his forehead that looks like an anchor, so he is our anchor for the time being.

Sep 14, 2010
Dear family and friends,

Matthew is at Hopkins PICU and under their care.

Thank you to Akron Children's Hospital. Hopkins may have a great reputation, but they cannot possibly be any more compassionate, harder working, or more dedicated than you. I will miss you all very much and promise to bring the boys back, especially Matthew, so he can slap the nurses that catheterized him. I told him he gets one free slap and the nurses said they'd gladly take it.

Chapter 6

"**B**rian! Can I borrow you for a minute?"

As a News Director, Kelly Groft wasn't much of a yeller. It wasn't her leadership style, nor did it fit the current climate of WMAR-TV. The legacy station, long removed from its golden days in television, was now trying to fight back and again contribute to the American narrative like it did sixty years ago. With Groft at the helm, her much leaner, but dedicated, crew was focused on telling the stories that mattered.

"I have a story for you," she said to me.

"You know we have done some stories on that professor over at Stevenson University, Susan Slattery?"

"Yeah," I said, "We just ran something last week right?"

"Right. She was incredibly popular at Stevenson and there's been a pretty impressive outpouring of support for her two children, who survived the crash, and her husband. The story is really heart wrenching. I've been reading the husband's journal entries on CaringBridge and I just tear up."

Kelly pointed to her computer screen, "I mean, Ed updates this thing two or three times a day, and hundreds of people read or comment."

While Ed had created the blog to keep family and friends updated on Matthew and Peter's progress, people, even complete strangers, began connecting with the powerful emotion he was conveying in his posts. The aftermath of the trauma settled over Ed like a thick fog, and he was using the blog to light his path out. It was evident to even the casual reader; a visceral and immersive narrative Ed built day in and day out. It was truly remarkable reading in that it was raw, personal, and unfiltered. Ed shared the most intimate details of his life and trauma, and allowed perfect strangers to sympathize, console and mourn with or for him.

"The family is finally back here in Baltimore," Kelly said, "Matthew is going through some intensive therapy over at Kennedy Krieger. Ed, the father, knows someone here at the station and wants us to tell his story."

"Really?"

"Yeah. The trucker fell asleep at the wheel and admitted it. It's a story Ed wants to tell, and I want you to tell it."

I hedged a bit, and explained how I already had a couple of stories going at the time that were more my beat. Crime, police...the gritty underbelly of Baltimore type stuff. I was a cops and courts guy and wasn't sure the Slattery story was my lane.

Ignoring my hesitation, she pushed a piece of paper across her desk. "Here is Ed's cell phone. He's expecting your call."

Kelly wasn't a rule-with-an-iron fist type boss, but I always knew when she meant business. I picked up that note and began to walk out of her office.

"Oh, and Brian," she added as she turned back to her computer, "I know this kind of story isn't your thing, but I feel you're the right one to tell it. Challenge yourself."

I called Ed almost immediately. It was an easy conversation, but I aimed to keep it brief. I knew he was dealing with a lot and I hated to be an imposition, but it was obvious this man on the other end of the phone wanted to talk.

"Sir, I am really sorry for what happened to you and your family," I said.

"Why?" he responded with a bit of levity, "You weren't driving the truck."

I was taken aback by his remark. As I searched for an appropriate response, he broke the silence with a chuckle.

"Don't be sorry, Brian. This isn't your fault. People say that to me all the time. 'I'm sorry, Ed,' or 'We are so sorry for your loss.' Do you know how many times I have heard that these past few months, Brian?"

Before I could answer, he did for me. "A thousand times. I'm just tired of hearing it because it doesn't meeeaannnn anything. Sorry? Sorry for what?"

"You know what, sir," I said, "I couldn't agree with you more. I really hate that, too, and I'm sorry for saying I'm sorry."

We both laughed, but more importantly, I began to get a brief window into who Ed Slattery was.

"It sucks is what it is, Brian. That's a word that counts here. It just sucks."

"Yes, sir," I said, "And I hear you want others to know it, too. I'm told you want to do a story with us about what happened."

"I do. I want to have you guys come down to the hospital here and see what is going on. We can talk and then you guys can go off and do your TV thing. I trust you guys to tell the story how you see fit. I just want to get it out there."

This man on the other end of the phone intrigued me. I knew immediately he was a rich character with a compelling story.

The Kennedy Krieger Institute sits just to the north of the Johns Hopkins Hospital campus in East Baltimore. A tunnel underneath connects the two institutions. Many of the children Hopkins cares for need special treatment by Kennedy Krieger, which focuses on pediatric developmental disabilities and disorders of the brain and spinal cord.

Matthew's traumatic brain injury certainly qualified, and he was transferred there from Hopkins after being received from Akron Children's Hospital. The twelve-year-old would be undergoing some incredibly intensive physical and cognitive therapy. It was standard belief at the time that there was at least a year window after suffering a traumatic brain injury in which patients could work back from the effects and regain some motor and cognitive skills. Therapy was crucial to maximizing whatever physical or mental capacity Matthew hoped to restore, and he still required 24/7 care. Even though the Slatterys were back in Baltimore, they were still living in a hospital.

So it was there where photographer Lamont Williams and I met to conduct the previously arranged interview. The hospital room we were directed to by the nurse was dark and quiet, but it looked lived in. Beyond the machines, hospital bed, tubes, and the other various medical accoutrements that tether a life to the sterile brand of hope, there were clothes, greeting cards, and posters with varying personal messages of 'Get Well Soon,' and 'We Love You.' On the far wall, there was a massive banner that read, 'We love you MACHOO!' written out by his classmates on one of those huge roles of paper from art class. It was hung at the foot of his bed and littered with signatures, personal messages of encouragement, and inside prepubescent jokes from his fellow twelve- year-olds.

It took all of ten seconds to realize we weren't just in a hospital room; we were in a living, breathing story of real people and real lives. It was all so immediately evident to both of us.

It was no mistake. This space was designed specifically to meet Ed and Matthew's needs. Since the first night at the Children's Hospital in Akron when Ed proclaimed that someone needed to be with his boys at all times, a movement began to take shape back in Baltimore. Alethea, the mother of one of Matthew's classmates, and a woman by the name of Anne Krach set up an online sign-up sheet for volunteers to take shifts watching over Matthew when he came back to Baltimore. They were to be four-hour shifts from early evening through the night until early morning to relieve Ed. People signed up. So many people signed up; acquaintances from school and church, good friends of the family, and the parents of kids Matthew knew from boy scouts. Even complete strangers donated their time in the wee hours of the morning.

The Slattery's community was rallying around the family, and not only offered to help, but desperately wanted to help. Even at the USDA, where Ed had only worked a few years, colleagues donated a combined year of their own sick time to the widower. It did Ed well to see these friends, family, and strangers sacrifice so much of their time. For a family that had lost so much, it was heartwarming to see how much people were willing to give.

In the weeks and months that followed the family's return, these volunteers not only donated their time, but decorations, books, and homemade signs and cards of encouragement. It all helped create that warm aura in an otherwise cold hospital room. It is what gave Ed the idea of yet another journal. He bought a simple single subject green Mead spiral notebook and left it in the room with a simple instruction that each volunteer write observations, messages, or whatever came to mind.

It gave Ed peace to read it in the mornings. Most of the messages were simple medical updates on how, or if, Matthew slept, if he moved a foot or a hand...or even if he seemed to react to a few hours of hearing a *Harry Potter* book read to him. Still, this notebook was a way for Ed to know what was happening when he wasn't there. It was a practical and pragmatic record of his youngest son's battle back, but it soon became messages of hope and a journal of an awakening; a compilation of good will and the kind of support a family can only dream of receiving from a community, who felt it had no recourse but to deliver kindness in droves. They took to calling themselves Matthew's angels and through the course of several months penned together vignettes of progress, hope and love.

September 14, 2010
6-10pm

Matt, welcome home to Baltimore. Mrs. Krach and I were thrilled to spend some time with you.

You were pretty tired from your trip and quiet most of the night. We chatted and told stories of how everyone at SJS is eagerly awaiting your return.

Yes, Timmy joined the choir, so now you need to decide....

We look forward to reading you some books, rubbing your hands and chatting more.
Much love,
Anne Krach and Carol Ellis Maychak

September 15, 2010
1:30am

Dear Ed,
Well, I've had the pleasure of sitting here with Matthew. He had a comfortable night so far.

Andrea is his nurse and she is awesome, very sweet, and loving.

I've been quietly talking with Matthew about all of the incredible community support and love surrounding him.

I know he is hearing my voice and I feel his Mom's presence with him.

Matthew you are so loved...
Kathy Sack

October 12, 2010
10:00pm

Ed,
I had the pleasure of meeting your Matthew tonight. I'm told by Jennifer that he had a visit from some therapy dogs that he enjoyed today...

He looks like such a sweet boy. He's just fallen asleep before I got here. I will keep praying for Matthew and your family. I'm planning to keep signing up for shifts and look forward to more time with Matthew.

Elizabeth Good

October 15, 2010

Chris the nurse tech was here with Matthew getting him cleaned and checking vitals.

Several guards directed me to the right place on my way here. One even guessing who I was because of the time of night. She remarked, "so many people love over that little boy."

How wonderful! The power of love!

November 13, 2010
6-10pm

I got here at 6:00pm and Matt is very sleepy. Kelli was here with Matthew and he was on Skype with Andrea in Japan. After Kelli left, Ms. Blevins, (Matt and I have her as a teacher) Mrs. Thornton, Maddie Thornton, Mrs. Krach and my mom and I stayed but now it is just my mother and I until 10:00pm. I held your hand, I told you stories, I hugged you and I did whatever I could to make you feel like the most comfy person in the world! I love you very much Machoo and NOBODY, and I mean NOBODY has treated me as nicely as you have. Keep on rockin' that sweet buzz cut brotha!

Love you bunches Matt!
Megan

One notebook became two and then three. The Slattery's community rallied around the family four hours at a time for seven straight months. Nearly 2400 hours and countless prayers were spent watching over Matthew as he began his long road back; a hopeful journey that was cheered on by the walls physically adorned with good will and faith. Standing in that room, even darkened by the dimming late autumn daylight, you could feel all of it as part of the story.

"They must be downstairs in therapy," the media liaison said to me, "Why don't you guys go ahead and set up while I go tell Mr. Slattery that you're here."

In an everyday rip and run news story, a crew would be lucky to use a light, let alone three point lighting, two microphones and filters.But this wasn't to be rushed, and if there was a photographer on WMAR's staff who wouldn't be rushed, it was Lamont Williams. He was one of the best in the business, and he took his time to set up the interview and frame everything just right.

As the chairs were angled and lights adjusted one last time, Ed walked into the room as if on cue.

"Mr. Slattery," I said immediately, "Brian Kuebler, from WMAR. It's good to meet you. This is Lamont."

We all shook hands and exchanged pleasantries, but Ed wasn't one to entertain vapid interactions; he didn't have time. There was an urgent meaningfulness about the way he conducted his conversations, while at the same time possessing a certain permanent disconnect about him, like a man who had not found the end of his pain. There was nothing post about his trauma and stress, which he wore on his sleeve and, more importantly, his face.

"So where do you want me?"

"In that seat is fine, sir."

"Oh Christ, don't call me sir, Brian, or Mister anything, for that matter. Ed. My name is Ed. Call me Ed."

A gentle smile grew on this face. I knew right then I would be able to break through the fog of the war going on in Ed's head to tactfully tell the story of this man, his loss, and the lessons he seemed handpicked to learn.

"We're good, Kueb," I heard Lamont say from over my right shoulder, the camera was rolling.

"So, Ed, I want to start by saying, ignore the camera, and the lights, and all the fancy equipment here. Really, this is just you and I talking okay?"

"That's fine," Ed said, already at ease. He was calm, confident, and ready to share with the world what happened to his wife and family, and why, perhaps, others needed to listen.

I only needed to ask the first question before Ed began talking, walking me through the crash, the injuries, the driver who fell asleep, and the journey his fractured family made back to Baltimore.

The interview was heavy and packed with the kind of visceral pain and acute emotion strangers rarely share with one another, but Ed didn't care. He had been through hell; there was a reason and he wanted people to know it.

Trauma affects people in so many ways. As a reporter, I have seen it countless times. Mostly, it's personal, private, and excruciatingly delicate, but for Ed it seemed to force a pivot toward a bigger calling; physically wearing his pain in the hopes that others never have to. His responses were so genuine, complex, and painful. It seemed as if he was unloading months of personal struggle off his shoulders and onto this tape rolling in the camera. It was equal parts therapeutic, refreshing, horrifying, revealing…and purposeful.

It was clear that just two months after a crash that killed his wife and permanently injured his youngest son, Ed Slattery felt he was wronged by a trucking industry run by profit, not safety.

While Doug Bouch was within his drive time limit when he fell asleep and killed Susan Slattery, Ed believed it was the pay by the mile structure and the 'time is money' mindset around which the industry was structured that aided in the fatigue.

Ed wasn't just making that pivot from victim to advocate, he was redefining it in a way I had never seen in all the stories I've told as a journalist.

Ed knew the facts he believed help lead to his wife's death and the argument against them by an industry he now had squarely in his sights.

"They say reducing hours for drivers according to sleep patterns will cost American consumers," he said in the interview, "that the cost of transporting goods will go up, and that will trickle down to you. Well," he continued, "that's a small price to pay, because the price I'm paying, the cost of having cheaper goods, I'm bearing that whole cost."

Ed stood still for a few seconds before settling back into his chair. As he did his hands gripped the wooden armrest, which made a noise. I looked down and noticed two rings on Ed's left hand.

I waited for him to fully settle. I watched his face. Ed seemed exasperated by his last comment. I could tell he didn't just believe the words he was saying; he truly felt the scorn in each and every one. I wanted to give him a break but I knew he had more to say. Two rings, I thought.

"Two rings?" I asked.

"Yeah, one is mine, the other is Susan's"

Ed was emotionless as he said it, as if it was just a matter of fact. And while it was to him, it signaled immense pain to anyone outside his world.

"Ed," I followed up, "have you even had a chance to mourn your wife?"

Ed pondered the question quite a bit before answering, "I suppose I haven't."

Ed's answer was so real and so personal that my next question was more of a human reaction than that of a removed journalist.

"Jesus Christ, Ed, how the hell do you deal with all of this?"

"You prioritize," Ed responded. "You get the best information you can, you make the decision, and then you live with it."

"You're doing a lot of living with it," I said.

"An awful lot of settling for," Ed said as he paused before compiling the rest of his thought, "and what I'm settling for stinks."

It was yet another one of those moments that transcends video; the kind of real, true emotion that boils the complexity right out of a story and into the hearts and minds of those who listen and watch.

Ed Slattery was, indeed, becoming an advocate, and his story was powerful enough to make people take notice.

"Well, do you want to see him? I want to introduce you."

Ed sprang up from his chair and the three of us were escorted downstairs to where Matthew had now moved on to physical therapy.

Ed jumped right in and helped the therapist.

"Matthew," Ed said in supportive tone, "This is Brian and Lamont. They are here to do a story about you."

Matthew was not responsive, or at least at that point didn't know how to be.

Medically, Matthew awakened from his coma just weeks before. It had been months. Matthew's brain was so terribly injured, he remained in a coma from the time of the crash until well into his stay at Kennedy Krieger in Baltimore. But, unlike a movie, he didn't just wake up. Coming out of a coma that deep is gradual and littered with countless false alarms, or what therapists call, involuntary movement.

It was voluntary movement Kelli and Ed were looking for night after night sitting by Matthew's side. The doctors said any stimulus is good stimulus, so father and daughter spoke to Matthew constantly, even swung the television on an articulating arm attached to the bed as close to his face as possible. Their tone certainly didn't suggest it, but their actions screamed WAKE UP!

It was a frustrating wait. Ed didn't know if Matthew would ever wake up again until one evening, the involuntary seemed voluntary. Matthew's head was still bandaged, his eye, even months after the crash was still bruised. Matthew's arm was resting on the arm of the bed when Kelli saw his hand move. Ed was not convinced that first night, but as Matthew began to incrementally improve, he continued to nudge his child awake. First was his hand and then, eventually, his eyes. Physically, Matthew was awakening to his new reality, but mentally was an entirely different plane he would need years to fully grasp.

Lamont and I saw Matthew not long after that initial moment. Matthew was undergoing intensive physical and occupational therapy to continue waking his body and mind.

The day we saw him, the therapist was working with Matthew to hold his head up straight for just seconds at a time.

I stood back and watched from afar, watched as this twelve-year-old boy fought so hard to accomplish basic movement. This child and his obvious struggle struck me, maybe more so by his father's decision not only to let me witness this, but to broadcast it. The responsibility to get this right began to weigh heavily, and I found myself struggling to come up with the beginning of this incredibly complex and powerful story.

"Go, go, go, go, go," I heard the therapist say as she was kneeled behind Matthew with two fingers on his forehead helping to pull back and lift his head.

As she pulled Matthew's head up, it was as if she raised his eyes to meet mine as I stood across from them. I looked right into them and, at that moment, I knew exactly how to start and end the script for his on-air story.

MATTHEW SLATTERY WILL TURN THIRTEEN ON THANKSGIVING...

HIS YOUTHFUL EXUBERANCE CAUGHT ON THIS VIDEO MONTHS AGO IS NOW, AT THE VERY BEST, HELD CAPTIVE BEHIND THESE FRUSTRATED EYES.

IT WAS AUGUST 16TH.

MATTHEW, HIS OLDER BROTHER, PETER, AND HIS MOTHER, SUSAN, WERE DRIVING BACK FROM A FAMILY REUNION IN CLEVELAND WHEN A SEMI TRUCK SLAMMED INTO THE BACK OF THEIR CAR AS THEY SLOWED FOR TRAFFIC.

SUSAN, A WELL KNOWN PROFESSOR AT STEVENSON UNIVERSITY WAS KILLED ALMOST INSTANTLY.

PETER WAS BADLY INJURED BUT STABLE.

MATTHEW'S DOCTORS SAY HE LOST EIGHTY PERCENT OF HIS BLOOD AND SUFFERED A TRAUMATIC BRAIN INJURY.

[The audience sees Ed working with Matthew in therapy] "Good job, buddy, see how long you can hold it...hold it hold it hold it. Excellent. Good job, buddy,"

THE PAIN MAY BE AS EVIDENT IN HIS FATHER'S EYES.

ED SLATTERY COULDN'T GO ON THAT TRIP TO OHIO, YET HIS LIFE WAS TRANSPORTED TO A PLACE HE WILL NEVER ESCAPE.

"You prioritize. You get the best information you can and you make the decision and live with it. *You're doing a lot of living with it.* I'm doing a lot of settling for and what I'm settling for stinks."

WHILE ED'S OLDER SON IS WALKING AGAIN AND BACK AT SCHOOL, ED'S WIFE, HIS CHILDREN'S MOTHER IS DEAD.

MATTHEW IS A GHOST OF WHAT A TWELVE- YEAR-OLD SHOULD BE.

MATTHEW'S ACCOMPLISHMENTS ARE LIMITED TO A SLIGHT NOD OR HOLDING HIS HEAD UP.

AN EPIC BATTLE BETWEEN MIND AND BODY IS RAGING IN THIS CHILD, BLISSFULLY UNAWARE OF WHAT HAPPENED.

HIS FATHER IS FIGHTING HIS OWN WAR ON REALITY, GRIEF, AND, AT TIMES, DESPERATION.

"There's no compensation, there's no amount of grace on this planet that can compensate for losing my wife, more importantly, my children losing their mother. I try to hold on to the graces, I try to recognize the graces, but I also know they are not enough."

BECAUSE NONE OF IT HAD TO HAPPEN.

THE TRUCKER WHO BARRELED INTO THE SLATTERY FAMILY ADMITTED TO POLICE HE FELL ASLEEP AT THE WHEEL.

WHILE FINAL REPORTS ARE STILL PENDING, INVESTIGATORS FOUND THE TRUCKER WAS STILL WITHIN THE LIMITS OF DRIVE TIME ALLOWED BY FEDERAL LAW.

BUT IT IS THAT STANDARD EXPERTS SAY KILLS TWELVE TO FOURTEEN PEOPLE A DAY.

"These are rolling time bombs. Every time you see a truck on the highway you have no idea whether a trucker has been driving for five hours or fifteen hours."

JOAN CLAYBROOK IS THE FORMER HEAD OF THE NATIONAL HIGHWAY TRAFFIC SAFETY ADMINISTRATION AND A WELL KNOWN ADVOCATE FOR REDUCING THE HOURS TRUCKERS CAN DRIVE.

CURRENTLY THE REGULATIONS DICTATE TRUCKERS CAN DRIVE NO LONGER THAN ELEVEN HOURS WITH TEN HOURS OFF.

BUT THOSE REGULATIONS COULD CHANGE BY AS EARLY AS NEXT YEAR.

AFTER SEVERAL SUCCESSFUL LAWSUITS BY SAFETY GROUPS, THE FEDERAL GOVERNMENT IS CURRENTLY LOOKING AT HOW MANY HOURS A TRUCKER COULD DRIVE IN ANY ONE GIVEN SHIFT.

THAT PROPOSAL COULD BE MADE PUBLIC ANY DAY NOW AND IT COULD BE THE NEW STANDARD IN THE INDUSTRY NO LATER THAN NEXT JULY.

"We think there will be a substantial change in the rule but we don't know. And if there isn't, then we are going back to the courts," the audience heard Claybrook say.

ACCORDING TO A STUDY BY THE NATIONAL TRANSPORTATION SAFETY BOARD, UPWARDS OF 40

PERCENT OF TRUCK FATALITIES ARE CAUSED BY FATIGUE, 4,000 AMERICANS DIE EACH YEAR.

CLAYBROOK'S GROUP DOESN'T BLAME THE DRIVERS THEMSELVES, BUT THE PAY-BY-THE-MILE STRUCTURE SHE SAYS ENCOURAGES GOING FASTER AND DRIVING LONGER.

"These are sweat shops rolling down the highway. Truck drivers don't have the control that they should, they don't get paid how they should, and they work extra long hours, and they exhaust themselves, and we're the people who are the victims."

THE AMERICAN TRUCKERS ASSOCIATIONS DISAGREES SAYING THE CURRENT DRIVING REGULATIONS WORK FOR THE MOST PART AND HAVE RESULTED IN A 20 PERCENT DECREASE IN FATAL TRUCK CRASHES LAST YEAR.

THE GROUP ALSO CONTENDS REDUCING DRIVE TIME HOURS WILL COST AMERICANS MORE FOR THEIR GOODS.

BUT THE COST TO ED'S FAMILY IS QUITE LITERALLY MORE THAN HE CAN BEAR.

"That's a small price to pay because the price I am paying, the cost of having cheaper goods, I am bearing that whole cost," the audience heard Ed say.

WITH LITERALLY A LIFE AND HIS CHILD'S INNOCENCE. IN BALTIMORE, BRIAN KUEBLER, ABC2NEWS.

Ed Slattery's words, his emotion, and his pure, unwavering character of wanting to right what he thought was such a terrible wrong was an empowering narrative.

At twelve years old, Matthew was learning everything all over again; at fifty-two, so was his father, and their journey would not only help heal them, but also be a vehicle for change. It would be a long road, but Ed saw no other path. He decided right then and there that he couldn't do it alone. The television story catapulted the Slatterys into living rooms all over the country, but he decided to continue telling his story every day thereafter, the story of him, his two sons, and the wife he had yet to mourn.

"Dear Family and Friends," Ed began to write on his CaringBridge blog, "I have decided to address my postings to Susan from now on. Don't know why, but here it goes."

What followed was an ongoing intimate, touching, and heartbreaking dialogue between a man and his deceased wife; a living record of the life and lives they architected. Ed Slattery was forced to begin a journey without his soul mate, but he still felt Susan needed to know every step, especially the day their youngest boy smiled again.

Nov 18, 2010
Dear Susan,

So, today was a great day. Our little boy really laughed today, I mean belly laughed. Miss Heather was blowing raspberries at him as she smacked herself on both cheeks with Matthew's hands. You should have seen him. I couldn't believe it.

Then, in OT, I told Miss Kelley and Miss Molly that the way to get a young teenage boy to laugh is to fart. Miss Kelley then told me that there is a fart app for the iPad. I found 'fart for free' at the iStore and downloaded it onto my iPad.

It has 16 different fart buttons and the therapists and Matthew played with it for the entire hour. He laughed and pushed the buttons on the iPad. We all laughed and laughed as we tried all of the different fart sounds. It was hysterical, and he showed the first signs of emotion since the crash. It was wonderful.

Well, I'll write again tomorrow night.

I love you,

Ed

Chapter 7

Ed retained Jeff Burns as his attorney shortly after the crash. Burns was part of Dollar, Burns, and Becker out of Kansas City, Missouri, and one of the leading attorneys specializing in truck driver fatigue.

Ed didn't know much in those first few days, but he knew that the driver, Doug Bouch, admitted to an Ohio State Trooper that he fell asleep at the wheel and that Jeff Burns seemed like the guy who could help him.

The Midwest lawyer had been litigating trucker fatigue cases for the better part of 30 years, and as tragic as Ed's story seemed to be, it was not nearly the first, nor altogether unique. It was why within just 36 hours of the crash, Burns and his partner Tim Dollar flew to meet Ed, Matthew, and Peter with a videographer and accident reconstruction expert in tow.

As Ed, Jeff, and Tim were having their first meeting, the videographer and accident reconstructionist were driving the route of the accident to document how it all happened. The pair recorded that route along Interstate 80 near Streetsboro, noted distances between construction warning signs, length of still fresh skid marks, and the charred jersey wall from where Bouch's rig burst into flames. They also obtained police reports and made sure each vehicle was impounded. Beyond the physical evidence on the road, it was also important to document the injuries. Peter and Matthew were both filmed to document their trauma and the decidedly longer, more treacherous road, in front of Matthew. The team performed the rapid, but rigid, due diligence in order to leave no room for any interpretation, and all of it within a day and a half of the crash.

It was one of the reasons why Ed felt he hired the right guy. Beyond his experience, Ed could see Jeff had a real compassion. It was easy for Ed to feel that Jeff was truly moved by his circumstances, that he wasn't showing the shallow or disconnected sympathy attorneys are generally paid handsomely to at least manufacture. Jeff Burns had genuine human empathy he wore on his face, and it was a face Ed instinctively liked. So much so, that Ed put whatever there was to salvage from his family's life into Jeff's hands, and Jeff began piecing it back together around the giant hole left vacant by Susan's life and Matthew's condition.

Jeff's investigation was not so much about what happened as it was about the impact it had on the Slatterys. If there were criminal charges filed against Bouch or the company he drove for, well that was a separate matter, one that would ultimately be determined by a grand jury in Portage County, Ohio. Jeff was pulling together what he needed for a civil suit. He was interested in damages; how did this crash damage the Slatterys.

For that he needed to interview doctors, assess prognoses, and determine just how much money it would cost to care for Matthew through the rest of his life. Burns was trying to determine what it would cost for a life care plan, trying to make dollars out of what didn't make much sense. If everything, indeed, has a price, so then does the life lived between the very moment Matthew was robbed of his innocence and the day he will ultimately die.

To a man whose life's work was numbers, solving for x never seemed so morbid, but it was expected and calculated often in cases like the one Jeff was building. What was not as emotionally digestible was how the economist his team hired calculated the worth of Susan's life.

As intelligent of a species humans can be, we are equally, if not more, emotional. To calculate an actual figure, the free market value of a life seemed cold and arbitrary but Ed intrinsically understood the sterile science of it all. Ed knew emotion didn't figure. He knew everything, indeed, had a price. It was a lesson he could recall teaching his own students when they would react emotionally to his lesson on the very same subject.

"Ah, but you can put a price on a life," Ed would lecture over the groans, "Listen, we can agree that a life is not worth zero, but is one life, say, equal to the national gross domestic product of the United States?"

Getting his students to suspend emotion for just a minute, the question seemed ridiculous. Maybe, just maybe, a life does have a price tag.

In the confined realities of a written lesson plan, the economic theory squared. It made complete sense minus emotion. Never did Ed realize he would have to add up the value to someone in his own life; never did he think he would have to take a calculator to someone he loved.

Susan's life was worth six million dollars.

The figure was not arbitrary. There was a formula applied, and it was one Ed knew. Take Susan's life earnings, add her career trajectory, project outward, and assume a promotion to Dean at Stevenson University. Figure in cost of living increases and then, somehow, monetize the value of parenting. Compute and then apply a dollar amount to the things that moms do in this life. How much is bandaging Matthew's skinned knee worth? What about advice she gave Peter on his first crush? Better still, what is consoling him after his first break up worth?

All of it has a worth, we know that as sons and daughters, we know that emotionally, but it also has a free market value—a number.

Susan's was six million dollars. The life of Susan Palmer Slattery would fetch 1.8 million for her economic loss and 4.2 million for the emotional loss.

But at this early point, a $600,000 advance would have to be enough.

Estes Express Lines knew it would likely have to settle with Jeff and the Slatterys. While the criminal investigation was certainly still pending, the evidence already gathered was stark enough. Estes gave the Slatterys just more than a half-million dollars while it worked with Jeff Burns on a final settlement. It was money to take care of immediate medical needs, needs that were becoming incredibly clear with each passing day at Kennedy Krieger.

Matthew, having just turned thirteen, had been receiving intensive physical and cognitive therapy for two months at the hospital, and was improving. Much to Ed's unmitigated delight, there was no longer a lost look in his eyes. Ed could see the light behind his son's eyes again, but he also saw Matthew battling with his brain to accomplish the simplest of movements.

Matthew was now able to hold his head up on his own. Still not able to speak, he could communicate in short staccato style bursts of noise or muster facial expressions, like raised eyebrows and, more importantly, an occasional laugh. It was the kind of laugh Ed wished he could put on repeat and play on an endless loop. That laugh was familiar, and it signified a pulse from the beautiful kid stuck inside that injured body.

Mentally though, he seemed capable of much more. Matthew's eyes began to clue his father in to the frustrating but lively dialogue that was racing through his brain looking for a way out. At times Ed could almost see Matthew's thoughts were trapped, bouncing around and looking for a way out. It was maddening at times, but Ed knew those thoughts were there, and that, he thought, was a victory itself.

Matthew's body lagged, but his brain was healing. Ed could feel it and see it with his boy's growing understanding of humor and the complexity of it. It was a magnificent sign of progress, even if the material was almost entirely about farting or comedian Jeff Dunham.

Dunham, a ventriloquist, cracked Matthew up. He liked the comedian's bit with the puppet Achmed, the Dead Terrorist. It simply slayed Matthew, so much so, Ed and Matthew's therapist had the idea of using Dunham's routine in therapy.

Matthew's right hand was practically useless, but his left had promise, and the therapist thought if she could work the teen hard enough, he could regain the use of at least one side. So she concocted a switch mechanism. She placed it just out of reach of Matthew's finger and, if he could trigger the micro switch by moving his finger, it would play Jeff Dunham's act on a small screen.

Matthew would stare at that switch, then his left hand. He would stare so hard, so intently, that when Ed looked into his son's now expressive eyes, he could see the battlefield on which Matthew's brain and motor skills were engaged in this bloody war. It bested Matthew for days. Each attempt more tiring than the next, until one day, his left finger started to quiver ever so slightly before resting. The look in his eyes was a mix of disappointment and concentration. Then, again his finger quivered, but this time, just a bit more. Finally Matthew's finger moved just enough to trip the micro switch.

"Good evening, Achmed," Dunham said as the bit began.

"Good evening, Infidellll!"

A smile started to crawl along Matthew's otherwise-paralyzed face, either because of comedic material, or because of the satisfaction that he just won a battle. Only he would ever know.

Matthew would need to continue to battle for months under the careful eyes of around-the-clock care, but there was a limit to what insurance would provide, and five months was where that line was drawn.

The progress was remarkable and encouraging, but Ed knew there was still so far his little boy could go. The staff at Kennedy Krieger was bringing Matthew back to life a little more with each challenge. It was progress Ed saw and participated in every day. Ever a realist, Ed knew it was a matter of time before the insurance company would feel enough milestones had been met and that Matthew should transition to in-home care.

Wanting Matthew to be well enough to be discharged was one thing, but Ed was simply not prepared to welcome home a disabled son who needed 24-hour care.

The family's old apartment was no longer suitable for this new life, so for weeks, when he could slip away for a few hours, Ed tried to find a new home for his family. It wasn't easy. He didn't want to cause Peter any more stress by moving far away, but the house had to be wheelchair-accessible. Eventually, Ed found a single-family home to rent in Cockeysville, Maryland, north of Baltimore. It had a wheelchair ramp and was close enough to their old apartment. But beyond a new home, Ed knew he needed so much more, not the least of which was a hospital bed for Matthew, a night nurse, and a myriad of other incredibly expensive equipment.

While the family had the army of volunteers helping him with Matthew in the hospital, no one could guide him on how to bring that hospital care to a private bedside.

Ed needed, he desperately wanted, a heads-up from the hospital or the insurance company as to when Matthew would need to be discharged. There were a lot of moving parts and, as long as he had that heads up, he knew he'd have time.

Ed was assured he would get that notice, until, well, he didn't.

It was a Wednesday afternoon when Ed walked into a room inside the hospital with maybe twenty people sitting around a table. There were doctors and nurses and physical therapists, all flanked by people from the insurance company.

They told Ed Matthew would have to be discharged that Friday.

"This Friday?" Ed asked before erupting. "Ya know, you're throwing me under the fucking bus here! I don't have a hospital bed ordered yet, hell, I don't even know how to put a catheter in him, or change any of those damn tubes!"

It was insane. He stormed out and went straight to Matthew's room. Matthew was downstairs getting the kind of therapy Ed knew was helping, but was just told was about to end.

Pacing back and forth, the normally mild-mannered and patient man became angry and, in an uncharacteristic fit of rage, spotted the meatball sub he ordered for lunch. He picked it up, wound back like Nolan Ryan and hauled that sandwich against the wall, violently splashing marinara sauce all over the room. It looked like a crime scene, but there was nothing figurative about the injustice Ed felt like he was being dealt.

Absolutely no one judged him. The doctors and nurses had seen it many times before. A nameless and faceless bureaucracy seemingly made an arbitrary decision that Matthew's 24-hour care was over. Ed felt powerless to fight. In his mind it was yet another tragic wrong, another event in which he had no control. It was perhaps the first time since the crash Ed lost control.

The next day Ed walked into Kennedy Krieger with a platter full of meatball sandwiches. He called it a mea culpa, but everyone on Matthew's team understood, as they often dealt with that violent clash of insurance bean counters and real life suffering. But Ed's marinara meltdown proved effective, Matthew would get a stay of discharge and continue his therapy for another month. Ed took that time to prepare for Matthew's homecoming.

It was a modest house on a large lot. It was technically a split-level, but the access to downstairs was a spiral staircase. Most importantly it had a ramp out front, and the first floor had a bedroom big enough for Matthew's hospital bed, a small kitchen, and a living room. It wasn't the ideal home Ed had hoped for, but having all of that on one floor was critical to Matthew's care and mobility. For this next phase of their journey, it was home, and on a cold winter day, Matthew saw it for the first time.

The thirteen-year-old hadn't seen the outside world in six months. Receiving various levels of care since the crash, Matthew's world consisted solely of hospital beds, beeping machines, nurses, and the ambient clatter of sterility that is always present outside a hospital room door. Finally, he would be leaving that world to begin his new life. Ed felt that was a big deal, and wanted it to be documented in a follow up news story.

~~~

It was early February when Matthew was discharged. While not a winter with a lot of snow, it had been bitterly cold in Baltimore. On that day the wind was whipping. It was the kind of raw cold that reminded your face February may be the shortest month, but it was winter's cruelest.

Matthew was bundled up and wheeled out of the hospital's main entrance on Broadway where his father waited with a brand new handicap-accessible van. The wind howled as it cut through every person on that curb. While everyone else was focused on the many tasks at hand, bundling him up, lowering wheel chair ramps, locking the wheelchair in the fancy new van, and documenting these efforts on camera, I kept my eyes on Matthew.

I watched his face in the middle of all this organized chaos, and saw the boy turning his face into the bitter wind and smiling. It was a pure moment of experiencing a surrounding, like holding your hand outside the car window to catch the wind. Matthew was continuing to wake up to the world around him. While it was the dead of winter, the chill seemed to make him feel alive.

Ed was more concerned about the logistics of this new van. He ran around the vehicle and the curb mentally crossing off a checklist of how it all worked. He then got behind Matthew and rolled him into the van, locking him in place. They said goodbye to the nurses and doctors. Ed was thankful and appreciative, while Matthew was hamming it up from inside the van as he wildly waved before the pair headed north on Broadway to pick up the interstate that would take the family to their new home.

Ed explained every step in detail and continued talking to Matthew about the family's new home along the drive. While the teenager couldn't respond in full, or even sometimes partially, Ed knew he was capable of awareness and emotion. Matthew had made some incredibly significant progress while at the hospital, and he was becoming more and more expressive every day. Ed seized on that progress by making sure he was always speaking *with* his son and not *at* him.

It was that same gentle tone he used as he wheeled Matthew through each room of the new house.

"See, Matthew, this is the kitchen."

"And then, see here, this is the dining room."

All the while Matthew seemed to nod in recognition. Never really uttering anything, as he was capable of from time to time, but just nodding like a regular teenager patronizing his father. It was kind of like the traumatic brain injury version of a smarmy teen saying, "yeah, Dad, this is awesome. Where's my room?"

And then…they got there.

"And this here, Matthew…this is your room. Right next to mine."

Ed rested the wheelchair toward the window after doing a complete circle to show Matthew around his room. The thirteen-year-old saw the hospital bed, the machines, and the neutral white walls landlords always paint rental homes. He looked at all of it and, as blank as those walls were, the whites of Matthew's eyes burst with crushing sadness. Tears welled up before he emitted a loud, shuddering sob. Matthew didn't have full movement of his body, but his head and neck started writhing in deep sorrow.

"I know, I know. I know, honey," Ed said as he bent down to nuzzle his face into Matthew's. "It's okay, it's okay."

Ed held Matthew's head in a tight and warm embrace and spoke into the top of his son's still-scarred scalp.

"You miss Mommy, don't you?"

It was at that exact moment Matthew's sobbing became uncontrollable. He wailed under the now-full and oppressive weight of his mind finally waking up to the reality that his mother died in that crash; Mommy was no longer here.

"Me, too," Ed said cradling his son. "Every day, honey."

Feb 3, 2011
Dear Susan,

Well, we are home.

It was relatively easy but exhausting. There were tears all around, Matthew, nurses, doctors, even a few from me. I think Matthew was well aware of the situation. He also cried when we came into the house and when Peter came home.

ABC2 taped us leaving KKI and coming into the house. The reporter will come back next week for an interview. We'll have to see when they run the story.

There were about seven people here most of the day but now it is just Matthew, Peter, me and the nurse, Toni. She seems very good and was just brushing Matthew's hair. I will have to get used to doing most of his care because I can't afford this nursing care forever.

Matthew is laughing audibly at Big Bang Theory with Peter. We do not have TV yet so Peter hooked the Xbox up to the TV in Matthew's room. That will not stay that way but perhaps until we get the FiOS hooked up on Tuesday.

I can't believe I am sitting here with both boys under the same roof and both of them watching TV together. Peter keeps looking over at Matthew to see if he is reacting. He is very concerned about his brother. This is so good for all three of us and I know Kelli too once she gets home.

I love them so much. Thank you, thank you, thank you for the gift of Peter and Matthew.

I love and miss you every minute of every day.

Chapter 8

It took nearly a year for them to get here.

Ed Slattery and Jeff Burns sat at the giant table in a conference room tucked away at the Baltimore Marriott Waterfront Hotel. Legal aids, friends, and family flanked both men, but the main act was the two middle-aged men in the middle of one side of the table. Ed and Jeff bore a striking resemblance to one another physically, and both exuded a genuinely warm demeanor. Each had an approachable, affable, and soft edge that can easily trip a complete stranger into friendship. But this day wasn't about sharing a beer or telling war stories, it was about going to battle.

They were there early.

It was common practice for Jeff to get settled for a mediation well before the other side arrived. He liked to study a room, take note of detail, and make the client comfortable. If the sun was going to come in the window at a harsh angle, he chose the other side. If there were different kinds of chairs in the room, he would make sure his client had the most comfortable.

In this meeting room on Baltimore's Inner Harbor, the sun was inescapable. The windows were tremendous and the views of the Baltimore skyline were impressive. The chairs were standard issue for a typical conference room. They had a padded seat with a slight rocking back that always felt it might snap off at a moment's notice; the kind engineered to be comfortable for only forty-five minutes at a time. While he couldn't change the chairs, Burns could at least get Ed away from the sun and the distracting view of springtime on the Inner Harbor by choosing to sit with their backs to the windows. It was that same kind of attention to detail Jeff and his staff used to prepare for this mediation, a process that didn't just go back months, but more than four years.

Back in August when Ed Slattery retained Dollar, Burns, and Becker out of Kansas City, Jeff and his partner, Tim Dollar, immediately knew they had a case. The driver admitted to falling asleep at the wheel and the witness testimony in the state's accident report was damning, to say the least.

Douglas Bouch was on what is known to fatigue experts in the trucking industry as the 'first night back.' Line haul drivers, the kind of job Bouch did for Estes, work an early morning shift all week; up by 1:30 a.m., prepare the load at a pick up station, drive through the early morning hours to pick up a new load, and then retrace the route back again like a relay race passing the baton of American goods. These drivers max out the federal regulation for drive times and clock out after fourteen hours, but no more than eleven on the road. The schedule is adaptable, but on the weekends some drivers normalize their sleep routines to maximize time with family. It is the turn-around from Sunday into a new workweek that can prove most dangerous, and August 16, 2010 was a Monday, the first night back for line haul driver Doug Bouch.

With expert testimony on fatigue, the 'first night back' theory, Bouch's admission to dozing off and whatever else may have lurked on his driving record, Jeff knew he had a case.

But driver fatigue cases are never really about the driver.

When Jeff Burns found out Doug Bouch was driving for Estes Express Lines, he knew he didn't just have a case, he may have had a mandate for the trucking industry.

It was November 21, 2006 when Estes Express Lines truck driver Oliver Mitchell crossed the grassy median from northbound Interstate 85 in Oconee County, South Carolina to the southbound lanes, hitting Pamela Becker's car head on. Both she and her nineteen- year-old son Daniel were killed.

Jeff Burns represented Jeff Becker in the case. Much like Ed Slattery, Becker was the father and husband who was not in the car at the time.

The difference was, the driver in that case never made any statement about falling asleep. Instead, Oliver Mitchell and Estes Express Lines raised the defense of sudden incapacity. The carrier blamed the loss of control of the tractor-trailer on what is called cough syncope, a sudden and unexpected coughing fit that can result in losing consciousness.

Estes believed this rare condition removed the liability for the accident and prepared to argue as such in federal court. Jeff Burns certainly could not prove negligence if Mitchell had a sudden and unexpected medical emergency, but he prepared to punch through that defense by proving Mitchell didn't suddenly cough himself into unconsciousness. Medical experts were on standby to testify exactly how one suffers from cough syncope and how a person suffering from it would still have the time and wherewithal to slow the vehicle they were driving.

It was Burns's position that Mitchell suffered from fatigue and fell asleep at the wheel. Twenty-five depositions later, Jeff felt he had his case of a known danger in the trucking industry and the negligence of Estes Express Lines in addressing it. It was a case no more succinctly expressed than in just two of those depositions with a woman named Janice Beacham.

Beacham was the Risk Manager for Estes Express Lines. On June 28, 2007, she sat down with Jeff Burns for a videotaped deposition that would prove to be just as useful then as it did four years later.

Jeff wasn't seen in the video, just heard. In person, Burns spoke with a cadence that is reassuring, welcoming, and easy. But in this deposition, he was clinical and exact; choosing his words meticulously, robbing him of his typical warmth.

Beacham, for her part, sat at the end of a nondescript table in a drab-colored room. Her curly blonde hair framed a face that seemed perpetually caught between thoughts of what she had to say and what she may have wanted to say.

After getting Beacham to agree fatigue is the number one safety issue in the industry and that 'first night back' can present a dangerous situation, Jeff started down a line of questioning that would be the outline of the Becker case.

"To your knowledge at this point, other than posters and safety meetings that you talked about," Jeff began, "does Estes currently have any comprehensive fatigue-management training that it provides to its drivers?"

"Not currently, no," Beacham said as her eyes conveyed an almost grim anticipation to Jeff's questioning that seemed to be carving a line in concrete, rather than just sand.

"Has there been discussion of developing fatigue-management training for drivers?"

"Something more in-depth than we do? Yes."

"What discussions have been held on that?" Jeff followed up.

"I am not privy to..." Beacham paused, "I'm sorry I don't have the knowledge as to anything in-depth, but I do know it's slated for program."

"And how long have those discussions been a topic of discussions?"

"Within the past twelve months," Beacham responded.

"You are aware, aren't you," Jeff said, as if to circle his point, "that other motor carriers have comprehensive fatigue-management training that they provide to their drivers?

"Yes," Beacham said, while maintaining a kind of defensive posture that flinched with each truth under oath.

Jeff knew what he recorded in that legal record would help him build the negligence argument. Estes didn't have a fatigue management program for its drivers other than occasional meetings and posters hung in their offices around the country, the kind of posters, when hung next to other federal work place statutes, can often fade into the background like tired wallpaper in an old kitchen.

But Jeff wouldn't stop there. He pushed toward another oversight in Estes that could help prove a pattern of negligence.

Sleep apnea is another major concern for the trucking industry, a hazard that can easily impair a line haul driver. It was a theory Estes's risk manager agreed with on tape.

"Does Estes have a program under which it screens its drivers for sleep apnea?" Jeff asked Beacham.

"No."

"Have you read in the literature that many companies do screen their drivers for sleep apnea?"

"Yes."

Pressed further, Janice Beacham told Jeff under oath that Estes had various discussions about implementing a sleep apnea program, too, but it never materialized.

Jeff went on to record Beacham's admission that Estes also had no assessment plan in place to identify drivers at high risk of fatigue dangers or that the company didn't employ any of the safety technology used to monitor drivers, driver evaluation devices that could record drifting, hard braking, or speeding.

Beacham testified to all of it and, while at times hesitant, she answered all of Jeff's questions. While just one small part of his deposition process, the risk manager's testimony laid a pretty solid foundation on which Burns built his case.

Still, it was a case Estes's insurance companies seemed to want to argue in 2007. Negotiations stalled originally and the court date was fast approaching.

But the gavel never did fall in the Becker case. The motor carrier insurance representatives eventually agreed to settle. Most of the details remained undisclosed and confidential. The public would never know how much money Estes Express Lines and its insurers would pay out to Jeff Becker. No one would know the intricacies of the case Burns built and what may have been the linchpin that convinced the motor carrier to settle.

All of it was confidential except, as it would turn out, Janice Beacham and her testimony.

Jeff Burns resurrected the risk manager's 2007 deposition to be evidence in Ed Slattery's argument against Estes. Her four-year-old words were now part of Ed Slattery's suit and there would be no confidentiality clause negotiated in his case.

From the side of the table where Ed Slattery was sitting, there was nothing confidential about it.

Chapter 9

The door clicked and opened and, in the brief second it took for someone to appear, time froze. Like a major league baseball pitcher at the apex of his windup, there was a unique, still suspense present before a violent flurry of action.

One by one, suits came filing into the room, each pulling up a seat on the other end of the table. Perched at the head and in the middle, was the mediator.

The lines were certainly drawn between Estes and Ed Slattery, now it was about artfully toeing and two-stepping so they eventually intersected at a number Estes could live with and Ed Slattery's decimated family could comfortably live on.

At the reigns of that legal wrangling was the mediator. Typically, Burns liked to choose a mediator that is credible for the defense and, as a practice, always asks them for a list of three candidates. After diligent research, Burns chose a mediator out of Ohio. As most do, he started off with a typical spiel about how mediation is the last chance for both parties to have control over the outcome, that you can make the decision as to how this case would be resolved. Otherwise, it would be up to a jury, which is always a crapshoot. This case was slightly different, though. Ed was almost eager to go to trial. He wanted badly to let the world in on the last several months of his life, if only so it could see, bear witness to how this could happen to anyone. But in this moment, Ed's role was to remain quiet and watch Jeff put on a presentation that would convince the insurance companies on the other side of that table that they were prepared to do just that, if needed.

After formal introductions and empty niceties that, for a moment, eased the magnetic polarization of human sympathy and cold economics, Jeff started with how most negotiations end.

He explained they would not agree to a confidentiality clause as part of any deal the two sides may reach.

Jeff made clear it wasn't on the table.

Typically, the confidentiality clause is asked for by the defense at the very end. The plaintiff is usually about to settle for a large amount of money and the insurance companies would rather not publish the number or the details used to calculate the figure. While Jeff made a habit of always negotiating against the clause, many clients don't normally contest them, but Ed Slattery was not a normal client.

Ed had been researching, studying, and learning everything he could about the safety record of the trucking industry, including how it could be blamed for nearly four thousand deaths on American roads each year. "That is like a 9/11 each and every year," he would say, a refrain he would repeat to all who would listen. He also knew that while the United States Department of Transportation says fatigue is the cause of less than ten percent of fatal crashes, independent studies put those numbers much higher. Crashes and deaths due to fatigue is a woefully underreported issue and Ed wanted to shine a light.

It was not as if he didn't understand why the hours were set up the way they were. Being an economist he intimately understood the cost of transporting goods from one coast to the next and from one border to the other, but it was costing lives, including his own. No, there would be no confidentiality clause; Ed Slattery wanted the world to know how his wife was killed and about the industry he says killed her.

Sitting on the other side of the table, representatives for various insurance companies didn't flinch at Jeff's first salvo. He was confident Estes would settle and, even more confident, Ed would get a favorable if not historic settlement. Dollar, Burns, and Becker had been preparing for the negotiations as if it was a trial, and when Jeff stood up, he argued like an expert lawyer in front of an attentive jury.

Burns directed the room to focus on a PowerPoint presentation. The first slides were of the Slattery family. Ed, Susan, Peter, and a young, vibrant Matthew Slattery were all pictured smiling and happy. The insurance companies needed to see what was real life before it became surreal.

The next slide began to show the very last moments of that life in animation. The group watched as a 3-D mock up pictured a triple trailer truck barreling toward slowed traffic and plowing all of the vehicles in its path before coming to rest against a jersey wall and catching fire.

It visually depicted how forensics and eyewitness accounts said the crash unfolded. It took Jeff's firm months to get the animation correct and to scientifically demonstrate the physics behind the wreck, but it was Ed's last edit that made it more emotional. Some weeks before the mediation, Ed suggested they place the Estes logo on the animated truck.

As the animation came to a rest it dissolved into dash cam video of the first responding trooper. The carnage was clear by the thick, black smoke billowing into the August afternoon sky. Accompanying the images, the audience heard scanner chatter and 911 calls edited by Jeff's team. The visuals combined with a cacophony of trauma jarred the senses until it all faded to just one man's voice.

"When we first approached the truck the rear trailer was fishtailing and moving erratically. I felt so uncomfortable traveling with my wife and daughter, I didn't want to be anywhere near the truck."

Dr. Ronald Lee Zigler's voice grabbed the attention of the presentation much like a frustrated teacher raising his voice at the front of a raucous classroom.

He explained what he saw a mile or so back and how he wanted to and did pass the Estes triple. His eyewitness account continued as he explained what he saw in his rearview mirror, having passed Douglas Bouch, and then stopped at the construction bottleneck along the Ohio Turnpike.

"I began to hear the crash." "I told my wife and daughter we are gonna be hit and braced myself."

Dr. Zigler compared the noise to what he heard in news clips of the Iraq war. The crushing of metal sounded like an improvised explosive device in Iraq or Afghanistan. Sounds he likened to a war half way around the world were, at that moment, bearing down on him and his family.

"With truck drivers like this," Zigler continued, "who needs terrorists."

The sound bite from the telephone interview just hung there for a beat or two while the chaotic edits of the presentation to that point slowed and the background sounds potted down to a silence.

Fading up from silence and a black screen was Trevor Baughman sitting in a classic framed shot for a video interview. He began emotionally recalling the final moment before the crash from his perspective.

Baughman said he pulled onto the left shoulder to get out of the way. He remembered looking out his passenger side window and seeing the triple tractor-trailer fly by so fast, he compared it to a movie scene of a passing subway whizzing by a platform at full speed.

When the violence stopped, Baughman focused on a red Ford Focus. He said he saw the back left part of the car was struck and whoever was inside needed help. After running up to the driver's side, he said he could see Susan, slumped over into the passenger side, her chest still moving.

Baughman's words cracked and slowed in an attempt to fight off the inevitable physical emotion that accompanied recalling those traumatic images.

He recovered and explained how he ran to the other side of the car. "The one boy that was in front. He had blood coming from his nose," Baughman paused again, but in a more arresting and violently emotional way. He struggled to finish his description of a scene that, months later, still obviously haunted him, "It was seriously like a fountain."

He continued to testify along with interwoven sound bites of a passerby doctor who helped triage Matthew's injuries and perform the emergency care credited with helping save his life.

The presentation then cut back to Baughman who explained seeing Peter for the first time. He didn't even know there was another child in the car until Peter stuck his head up.

"He sat up," Baughman recalled in deep sorrow, "and he put his hand on Susan. Her chest wasn't moving anymore."

Peter didn't remember much of it. The presentation had cut to his interview for his recollection, as the sole surviving family member who could still articulate the experience. But even for him it was blurry. Peter was only shown detailing the flashes of memory he did have.

"I just remember the feeling of laying on pavement," he recalled with a periodicity that didn't necessarily describe his cadence so much as mimicked his memory in short vibrant flashes, "[people] shading me from the sun, feeling gravel in my skin. I remember the helicopter."

The emotional toll of the crash was tallied in tears and blank stares and grief-stricken breakdowns. The audience in that Baltimore conference room heard from Matthew's tween-aged friends now caught between the innocence of their teenage years and the brutal realities of adulthood. They described how their friend seemed trapped behind his own eyes, or that something was missing in their fragile little worlds, and that something was Matthew's infectiously loud laugh.

The insurance company representatives heard from Ed in the PowerPoint slides, too, as he was interviewed about his loss. Susan's parents were front and center telling their story as well.

"If you think about it hard enough, maybe it will go away and not be real," Susan's mother Ginger Palmer said. "It is no way to die."

Susan's father added to the sentiment, explaining how senseless Susan's death was, that it came while she was at the top of her life.

The emotional loss was adding up slide-by-slide, clip-by-clip, but just what was it all worth?

Love is, indeed, invaluable, but bellied up to a mediation table, it has a currency and a price.

Jeff made the case of what it was all worth. The formula lawyers and insurance companies used to figure such things started spitting out cold hard numbers on the screen.

Matthew's medical bills from the crash through February of 2011 totaled $981,722.99. The projected amount of money it would take to care for him the rest of his life was anywhere between 35 and 45.76 million dollars.

Then there was what Matthew lost in projected income in his life. It was figured based on level of education. A bachelor's would have netted him $2,698,379 over a lifetime. A doctorate was worth $3,804,035 and a professional degree about a million more.

Jeff moved on to Susan. The emotional loss to her family and community, notwithstanding, she should have earned 1.5 million dollars more in her career. The chores she did as a mom around the house were valued at just more than $607,000, totaling a real finite loss of $1,856,626.

Jeff then added Peter's medical bills and Ed's lost income from having to quit his job at the USDA to care for Matthew full time. Altogether, Burns said the crash cost the Slatterys anywhere between $40 million to just more than $53 million in cold, calculable cash.

The numbers were no surprise to those in the room. It was part of how mediations progress, but what wasn't as orthodox was how Jeff continued his presentation to sketch out just how he would prove negligence by the motor carrier if, indeed, they would go to court.

The very next slide read, "What if Estes knew?"

"Fatigue is a safety risk," the first line revealed. It was followed by the statistic, "31% of all commercial driver fatal collisions are caused by drowsiness." The third line appeared, "36% of trained drivers report nodding off during trips."

Jeff moved on to another slide entitled, "Estes grows." Burns detailed how the motor carrier grew in recent years to become the 18th largest transport company in the country. Revenues for Estes doubled from $700 million in 2002, to almost $1.5 billion in 2008, while adding nearly five thousand new employees.

Estes took off in the last decade and was still growing, Jeff argued, but maybe too fast.

Janice Beacham came up on the screen next. It was Jeff's old 2007 video deposition of her as part of the Becker case. Against the backdrop of everything the people in that room heard earlier in the presentation, the words from Estes's risk manager seemed heavy and saturated in context.

"Not currently, no," Beacham said on the screen.

No, there was no comprehensive fatigue management training for Estes drivers. The words carried an awful lot of weight for everyone at that table, because the one fact that was not in dispute was what Doug Bouch said to the state trooper in the police report.

Beacham's words were from 2007, but Burns was betting they would still support the argument he was about to lay on top of them.

Jeff clicked to the next slide. It focused on Doug Bouch. The document the room was looking at was Bouch's Medical Examination Report for Commercial Driver Fitness Determination from February 4, 2009. The Department of Transportation requires the exam every two years, and the copy on the screen was current at the time of the crash.

On the form, there were check marks next to two sets of symptoms: fainting or dizziness, and the experience of sleep disorders, pauses in breathing while asleep, daytime sleeping, or loud snoring.

Bouch's medical report also listed all the medications he was taking, including Prozac, Provigil, which is prescribed to patients with excessive sleepiness caused by disruptive sleep disorders, such as sleep apnea, and Topamax for migraine headaches.

The combination of side effects associated with Bouch's medications was in line with some of the symptoms checked earlier in his medical exam, such as dizziness and insomnia. Jeff also made note of the other side effects associated with those drugs, including vision loss and slowed thinking.

"No," Janice Beacham said in the next segment.

Jeff went back to his 2007 deposition of the Estes Risk Manager once more, this time picturing her saying no to his question of whether or not Estes had a program in place to screen its drivers for sleep apnea. Jeff also showed Beacham saying there was no real-time assessment plan in place to routinely identify those drivers at high risk, nor did the company employ any driver evaluation devices on its trucks.

Beyond the original hiring process, Jeff would conclude, as he prepared for his final point, that there was no living, breathing evaluation system in place to assess Estes's drivers.

Up on the screen appeared the final parts of his PowerPoint presentation entitled, "Bouch Driving Record."

Below the title were two separate infractions in October and then November of 2009. The first was for following too close and weaving, and the other for, again, following too close. Both infractions appear in the Estes company manual as symptoms of fatigue.

Then Jeff revealed the final piece of evidence he had from Bouch's personnel file obtained from Estes as part of a negotiated discovery process prior to mediation: Marked

February 17, 2010 was a document entitled "Notice of written warning from Estes." Jeff highlighted two handwritten quotes from the company document dated exactly six months and one day before Doug Bouch would kill Susan Slattery:

> "On two occasions, Mr. Bouch was observed with numerous safe driving violations. These acts represent a hazard to Mr. Bouch and the public and the company."

> "[He] must follow all safe driving procedures. Any future violations or observations will result in Mr. Bouch being removed from the triples operation."

Indeed, what if Estes knew? It was the question Jeff wanted to punctuate the room after his more than two-hour presentation. He wanted it to rattle around the brains of everyone seated on the other side of the table. What if Estes knew, and if it didn't, how and why not? Any part of an answer would imply negligence, and Jeff knew it.

Sitting at that table, Ed knew it, too. He was instructed not to speak or react, but he studied the faces across from him as each of Jeff's punches landed. Seeing it again and in this moment, Ed was equal parts impressed and incensed.

For the team Burns put together to tackle the Slattery case, that was the point. They worked tirelessly for eight months to create the presentation. They found witnesses police didn't, interviewed the doctor who helped triage Matthew at the scene, and dug into documents secured early on in the investigation. By the time Burns was ready to present, he was supremely confident he and his team were displaying Ed's case in the best possible light. An effort driven by the responsibility Jeff felt to take care of Matthew.

After Burns rested his argument, Estes and its representatives retreated to a different conference room. They had more people and paper and, obviously, a fair amount of discussion between Estes and its many insurance companies. Both sides were now in their figurative separate corners, and the negotiations began.

After a certain amount of time, a number was put on the table. The insurance companies representing Estes were prepared to offer $25 million. It would settle the case.

Jeff and his partner, Tim Dollar, immediately counseled Ed to reject the offer. For a company like Estes, there were several layers or tiers of insurance and while $25 million was the limit of Estes's first layer of defense, Jeff knew there was another level.

A settlement wasn't reached that day on Baltimore's Inner Harbor. Instead both sides left the city with what is called a high-low in the mediation game. Ed Slattery would be paid the first $25 million immediately, with the promise he would seek no more than $90 million if negotiations failed and the case ended up in court. This way Ed wouldn't get less than $25 million, and the insurance companies wouldn't have to pay out more than $90 million. The agreement left open the possibility of future negotiations; a possibility Jeff knew was a probability.

The high-low agreement meant not only would Ed and Matthew be paid up front, but so would Jeff, Tim, and their firm. Dollar, Burns and Becker stood to get paid handsomely out of that immediate money. The upper tiers of Estes's insurance protection knew that payday would only help to continue funding the case against them if Ed chose, enabling Jeff and company to go for broke upon failed mediation.

It was a month later when, predictably, both sides agreed to meet again, this time in Cleveland, Ohio.

The battle plan was still drawn up the same. Jeff didn't need to remind anyone in the room of the staggering case before them. There were no new surprises and, with $25 million already agreed upon, it could only get worse for Estes and its insurers if they would not negotiate in good faith, and everyone knew it.

A decision needed to be made. Either push the limits going for nearly $100 million or continue searching for a settlement. That decision was entirely up to Ed Slattery, who was very well aware he had an unbeatable hand in this tragic poker game.

Still, Ed didn't want to go for broke. He was never motivated by money. Susan wasn't coming back and the odds were, neither was Matthew as he knew him before the crash. What he was motivated by now was enough for a comfortable life for his disabled son and the open record of what happened and how. Resolving the case at this moment would be the best thing for his family and Matthew's future. Marching orders in hand, Jeff's team fired the first salvo at the previously agreed high point, $90 million.

In another room, Estes's insurance companies replied back somewhere at or near $30 million. Still not good enough Jeff advised Ed. "This case is bigger than that," Jeff would say.

Ed ended up rejecting $33, $35 and $38 million dollars, about $5 million past what he called his barf point. It was hard to reject those kinds of figures on the face of them, but the face Ed and Jeff needed to keep in mind was Matthew. The two knew what it would take to financially care for him the rest of his life, and whatever numbers were coming from the other side needed to be well above that figure.

Finally, Estes Express Lines's insurance representatives sent the mediator back to Ed's room with a number he and Jeff liked; $40 million. As a last condition, Ed asked for $800,000 more for Susan's family. Finally both sides agreed, $40.8 million.

It was a structured deal, involving cost of living increases and annual payouts through annuities, the kind of high finance not easily understood or managed but, in the end, figured to be worth more like $90 million over the life of the decision; Dollar, Burns and Becker would net a one-time payout of $13.3 million for the firm's efforts.

It was what is known in the law/mediation industry as a mega result. It was the highest ever recorded by Dollar, Burns and Becker but elevated even higher was the pain and suffering of the Slattery family and, as Ed hoped, the increased bounty for a motor carrier doing business by the mile. Beyond taking care of Matthew for the rest of his life, Ed wanted Estes to pay for the way he felt it was doing business on American roadways. For the company's part, there was not much in the way of friction or complications as the two sides headed for the historic settlement.

The process was fairly quick, mostly efficient and always civil, but Susan's death and the assault on Matthew and Peter's youth were still a criminal matter.

June 22, 2011 9:44am
Dear Susan,

So I am sitting in the Cleveland airport waiting to board in about 20 minutes.

Our business is settled. I can't discuss the details yet but it is of historic proportions and I am pleased with our lawyers and friends beyond anything I can express.

In the middle of our private hell, we are very lucky. Lucky to have the boys, lucky to have the friends we have, lucky that this wasn't an independent trucker with minimum insurance, lucky to have found the legal team we found, and even a little lucky that the trucking company was as cooperative as they were.

I will work on truck safety issues for the rest of my life. I don't know what form that will take but I will be in the fight.

I love and miss you,

Ed

Chapter 10

The print on the first page of Portage County Court of Common Pleas Case 2011CR0483 read like a loud bang. "INDICTMENT:" was written in very large, bold, block print followed by, "AGGRAVATED VEHICULAR HOMICIDE; VEHICULAR ASSAULT (2 Cts)."

The description just below it was written in a combination of italicized or bold print which explained in old and proper English what the grand jury thought was the first of ultimately three punishable actions against the peace and dignity of the state of Ohio.

"On the term of July in the year of our Lord Two Thousand Eleven," it started.

"The Jurors of the Grand Jury of the State of Ohio, within and for the Body of the County Aforesaid, on their Oaths, in the Name of by the Authority of the State of Ohio, do find and present that **Douglas S. Bouch** *on or about the* 16th *day of August, 2010, at the County of Portage, State of Ohio aforesaid did* **while operating or participating in the operation of a motor vehicle, to wit: 2006 Mack Semi Truck, Pennsylvania License No. LZ7599, cause the death of Susan P. Slattery, to wit: recklessly."**

The document was the True Bill signed by the foreperson, the written decision of the Ohio Grand Jury saying it heard sufficient evidence from the state to believe Doug Bouch probably committed three crimes, the reckless death of Susan and the vehicular assault on each Peter and Matthew.

The jury handed up that indictment and the document was stamped and filed on July 27, 2011. Grand juries are a secretive process in the Unites States. No one but the members of the jury and select prosecutors knew just what charges Bouch faced. The case against the truck driver, and perhaps his fate, was sealed and neither he nor the man his actions impacted most knew as July flipped to August.

Ed Slattery wasn't monitoring the court files of Portage County, Ohio. Back in Baltimore and fresh off one of the biggest settlements ever recorded against the trucking industry, he and his family were busy finding their new normal.

Matthew's progress was astonishing. Certainly not what he was before the crash. Physically, that Matthew died at mile marker 190 on the Ohio Turnpike, but mentally, he was steadily re-emerging, if ever so slightly. From behind once dead and frustrated eyes, now illuminated the vibrant hues of innocence Ed first thought might have been eviscerated in the violent wreck.

With the help of intense therapy Ed could now afford, Matthew continued to incrementally improve in the year after the accident. His ability to talk and even converse was progressing, albeit still in short bursts of gravelly sounding squawks and wails. At times, Ed thought his son could sound like the verbal equivalent of stubbing your toe; but what he lacked in articulate finesse, he made up with his expressive eyes. To Ed, it was as if his son's eyes flipped open like an old window shade, finally letting Matthew look out, and Ed to look in.

His boy wasn't just in there, Ed thought, he could see Matthew was ready to live this new life. Physically impaired as he was, Matthew's wit was sharp and cunning and refused to be muted by the patronization often afforded to the disabled.

It was small progress, but the kind Ed Slattery thought should be celebrated, not mourned, as the first anniversary of the crash approached. He convinced himself going back to Cleveland and Akron, and even to the very mile marker where his wife was killed, was essential to the family's healing.

Ed expected both his sons would react wildly different to his decision. Peter was nearly fully recovered physically, but was showing signs of struggling emotionally. Ed didn't quite know on what level Matthew would react, nor was he fully confident in what he would do. Ultimately, though, he knew the road back had to start where it once ended. While that was technically on Interstate 80, emotionally the journey would begin with the reunion of a fractured family along the gentle shores of Lake Erie.

Despite her death, or because of it, Susan's parents continued to host the annual get-together at their home in Rocky River, Ohio. While it would be bitter without Susan, it would also prove to be sweet by how much they still had in each other.

The Palmer family reunion was exactly where Ed wanted himself and his boys to be a year later. August 16, 2011 was a day he wanted to commemorate, and looked to punctuate that by a celebration far beyond the four walls of the Palmer family house. There were people to thank and gratitude to be shown, and Ed was now armed with the means to do it.

~~~

Ed booked an aggressive schedule for the day. It was planned out expertly and handled much like the itinerary of a dignitary, complete with a press liaison.

Ed Slattery invited me out to Ohio to witness and cover the day. This would be my fourth story on the family as my station continued to show interest in the family's progression through the previous year. Ed thought it was important to show people just how vital of a role community in both Ohio and Baltimore played in the ongoing recovery of his family.

The first stop was at noon at the Streetsboro, Ohio Fire Department. It was located due south of the part of the interstate where the crash happened exactly a year and fifteen minutes prior. The men and women of the Streetsboro Fire Department were the first responders on the scene, and were critical to saving Matthew's life. Ed wanted them to see just what they did.

As the family walked into the bay where the department kept its engines, Matthew, in his wheelchair, was in awe of the colors and the equipment, much like any 13-year-old boy would be. His emphatic and vivid eyes were cluing others into not only his interest in the firehouse, but also his buoyant personality.

"Guys," Ed said as he wheeled Matthew toward the group of first responders, "This is Matthew. Do you remember Matthew?"

The response was murmured, not for lack of memory, but just the opposite. Many of those men and women never thought the boy they pulled out of that car a year ago had any chance of surviving.

One by one they kneeled down and said hello to Matthew who smiled and waved from his wheelchair. He could only get out the word "Hello," but his facial expressions and nodding filled in the rest of his intent.

It was a communication and personality Ed knew in large part was thanks to the men and women standing in that garage, the group that acted quickly and saved both of his sons' lives, and, perhaps, even his own.

It was why Ed presented Lieutenant Kevin Grimm with a check; a donation to the Streetsboro Fire Department for $10,000, written out on a check that still read from the bank account of Susan Palmer Slattery and Edward Slattery.

Ed was paying it forward not only because he recently was awarded the means, but also because his gratitude had no end.

Lieutenant Grimm responded in kind by explaining how the department was making up a special plaque dedicated to Susan. It read, "In honor of the life and work of Susan Palmer Slattery." Lieutenant Grimm explained it would hang on the station's same memorial wall as fallen officers.

It was perhaps the first time Ed realized the crash of a year ago deeply affected lives other than his own family. It was a moment that quickly resulted in a long embrace between the two men. Ed was still wearing my microphone from his presentation of the check, and it was now buried between Kevin and Ed. The audio it captured was a deep and knowing sigh. Ed owed everything to the man, and he tried to make it evident in his lingering embrace.

It was a decidedly different scene as the caravan headed a half-hour south to the Akron Children's Hospital. Ed was giving back to the hospital, where he spent a solid month of his life, as the doctors saved the lives of his children. It, too, deserved his newfound financial gratitude.

It was a much more orchestrated media event. Members of the local press and television stations all turned out for the check presentation from Ed to the hospital. There was much pomp and circumstance bringing the family back to the hospital a year later. This time, all three Slatterys entered through the front door, not the roof entrance from a helipad. It was money well-spent when Ed stood up at the podium and presented the hospital a check for $100,000 to be used to provide therapy for children who otherwise wouldn't be able to receive it. Susan would never want their name on a building, so Ed gave the money and told the doctors to put it to a better use. He would rather cash in his gratitude with a smile from a sick child than having his or Susan's name on a hallway or wing.

For the outside observer it looked like an event that served to tie up the loose ends of a horrific crash many still remembered, but for Ed, it was chapter one of year two, and he expressed as much in his remarks to the crowd.

"Most importantly," he said as he turned to Matthew and Peter sitting with their cousins across the room, "it is a celebration of our boys, Peter and Matthew. Mommy and I love you more than you will ever know, and any parent knows what that feels like..."

Ever cognizant of a sound bite, the local reporters started jotting down the time code from their cameras marking this recorded moment. While other cameras were fixed on Ed, I panned mine toward Ed's boys. Both were looking at their father as if he was addressing only them in an empty room.

"Your mom shines through you every minute of every day," Ed said, locking eyes with his sons'. "I see her in your smile, I see her in your determination. Your mother worked harder than anybody I've ever known."

While the money and the spectacle of this staged event was clearly important for the hospital, Ed's words punched through all that clatter to connect with Peter and Matthew across the room. Beyond all the cameras and the bunting and the banquet tables, it was about just one message; that Ed's boys knew the prior year wasn't easy and, together, they could make the next year a little easier.

At the end of a long day, it was a message received. As the family and friends retreated out of the limelight and back to the Palmer lake house, I had just a few more questions for Ed. Ed explained again how he wanted his boys to mourn their mother, but he also wanted to celebrate how far they had come.

We ducked into an empty hospital room to do a formal interview, and as I was wrapping up what I thought was the last moment for the day, I noticed Matthew staring at his father while Ed responded to a question. It prompted one last question in a day that had been full of them.

"He looks at you…" I said gesturing toward Matthew.

"Whaaaat," Matthew said flipping up his palm, as if he was annoyed I had caught the intimate moment between father and son.

"Yeah. I feel this stare an awful lot," Ed said looking at Matthew, "I think we just look in each other's eyes and we just love each other. Is that right?" he asked.

Matthew nodded and said with a tired voice, "I know."

Ed smiled back at his son, "I know you know."

It was a tender moment. Ed was locked in a loving gaze, as if he was studying the pain of the last year in Matthew's eyes and devising how he could continue to fix it. Fatherhood is different now he thought. Ed found himself as a single parent again, but much later in life, and in a much more unique circumstance. Still, the love he saw reflected back at him in son's eyes validated his decision to return to Ohio; surrounding his boys with family and celebrating Susan's life could help heal from her tragic death.

It was just after dinner at the Palmer family lake house, and the family was winding down from a long and emotionally draining day. The entire family was on the back porch, including Jeff Burns, who had become close with the family. He was strumming a guitar and playing an acoustic and soft version of the Beatles "Hey Jude."

It quickly became a sing-a-long. It was gently-paced, so Matthew could follow along with Ed's direction. Again, father and son were locked in a soft and caring stare, as Ed willed Matthew to get the words out to the 60s classic.

"Take a sad song and make it better..." the family sang softly as they watched the brilliant late summer sunset on Lake Erie.

"Remember to let her under your skin, then you'll begin..." they paused. Ed and Matthew then took a breath to sing the last few words. Again, Ed was reading the map in his son's eyes, but this time, it was of a completely new terrain.

"Ready," Ed said quietly as they waited for the guitar. Matthew stayed focused on his father before, together, singing the last words of the song, and perhaps the first words of a new year, "...to make it better."

~~~

The next day, Ed was told Doug Bouch was indicted by a grand jury. It would be the only detail prosecutors would share with the widower until later that month.

On August 29, 2011 the Portage County Court of Common Pleas unsealed and delivered the warrant for Douglas S. Bouch to the sheriff's department. It was the day the criminal case against the truck driver would go public, and at 6:40 a.m., the warrant was served, and Bouch was arrested.

Later that afternoon, Bouch appeared before the court clerk, signing an agreement to be released as long as he complied with the court in the case against him. Otherwise, he faced a $50,000 bail, a hefty price to pay for what would end up being his last five months of freedom.

Aug 17, 2011
Dear Susan,

We take no joy in the announcement that the trucker who killed you has been charged for the crash that took so much from us.
I do not hate him, and even forgive him, but I believe that people should take responsibility for their actions. I also believe there is a deterrent effect to punishment that is desirable in a civil society.

That's all I will say at this point. I don't know what he was charged with, but I do know it was a felony indictment handed up by a grand jury.

I love and miss you and hope that you will watch over him and his family this day, especially.

Ed

Chapter 11

Six weeks later, Doug Bouch pleaded guilty.

It was a written plea for the court's consideration, and he admitted to each count in full; the aggravated vehicular homicide of Susan Slattery, and the vehicular assault to both Peter and Matthew Slattery.

For Susan's death, Bouch understood the penalty was five years in prison and a $10,000 fine. For the injuries to Peter and Matthew, he was looking at a total of three years and another $10,000. Bouch pleaded guilty in the hopes of reaching a deal with the state, but his fate would stay in limbo until the sentencing hearing scheduled for early 2012.

Ed Slattery got news of Bouch's plea, and was relieved he wouldn't have to put his family or Susan's family through any sort of trial. Both families had come such a long way since the crash, but it was still far too fragile to survive a weeklong onslaught of the emotional facts and details litigation would entail. Whatever would come of Doug Bouch would be determined a few months down the road, and it was a comfortable enough cushion for Ed to focus his attention on a different kind of battle, one happening on Capitol Hill in November.

Through the emotion and success of the civil negotiation, the year mark of Susan's death, and even the more recent developments of the admission from the man that killed her, Ed Slattery continued to pivot from victim to advocate.

He hadn't just been studying the issue of driver fatigue in the American trucking industry, he was becoming the face of it. Ed was active in the organization called Parents Against Tired Truckers, which operated under the Truck Safety Coalition. The

TSC was in the middle of an intense campaign advocating for reduced hours for truckers and Ed was ready to lend his family's story to that cause.

Late in 2011, the Obama administration through the U.S. Department of Transportation's Federal Motor Carrier Safety Administration was expected to issue a new service rule on the maximum number of hours commercial motor vehicle drivers were permitted to work per day, as well as the amount of rest between workweeks. The FMCSA was created in 2000 as a separate part of the DOT aimed at reducing crashes, injuries, and fatalities involving commercial large trucks and buses. The proposed 'hours of service' rule change would reduce a potential workweek for truckers by twelve hours. As it stood, truckers were able to work up to eighty-two hours in seven days, the FMCSA wanted to drop that to seventy hours, based on the latest research in driver fatigue and six public listening sessions throughout the country.

Part of this proposed rule change also created what trucking safety advocates believed was a key provision, a so-called 34-hour restart. The clause would make it so a trucker would get 34 solid hours of rest before starting a new workweek and those hours must include two periods from 1 a.m. to 5 a.m., the time most experts agree the human body reaches the most restorative type of sleep known as REM sleep.

The proposed rule change also included reducing actual drive time hours. It was no more than eleven hours in one day, but the government was studying the effect of limiting it to ten. All parts of the proposed rule change signified substantial progress by the FMCSA for safety groups; however a still newly elected Republican House of Representatives thought the pending regulation was overstepping, as evidenced in the title of the hearing under the U.S. House Subcommittee on Regulatory Affairs, Stimulus Oversight and Government Spending. It was called "The Price of Uncertainty: How Much Could DOT's

Proposed Billion Dollar Service Rule Cost Consumers This Holiday Season?"

In opening remarks, Chairman of the subcommittee, Ohio Republican Representative Jim Jordan, began the hearing with a statement: "This last week, ordinary people across these great United States have engaged in the annual tradition of shopping for Christmas gifts, rising at predawn hours to take advantage of Black Friday sales and Cyber Monday deals. The shopping season is vital to the survival of so many small retailers. The vast majority of all retailers and 80 percent of all U.S. Communities depend solely on trucks to deliver and supply the products sold in stores or ordered online. At last count, trucks moved $8.3 trillion worth of goods annually, facilitating nearly 60 percent of the economy."

But there is worry creeping into this American tradition, Jordan continued. It was a new regulation the Obama Administration was poised to sign into law, and it threatened to raise the price of goods, cut revenues, and jeopardize the fragile economic recovery. Jordan put the cost of the regulation at about one billion dollars a year.

The opening salvo also made mention of bipartisan concern about the proposed rule and the possible consequence of roadway congestion by forcing more truckers on the road at peak times to meet demand.

The platform of any discussion in the hearing was set, but before Jordan moved forward with introducing his panel assembled for the hearing, he yielded his time to the ranking member of the minority party, also of Ohio, Democratic Representative Dennis Kucinich.

Kucinich opened from a different position, discussing just how high the cost may be without proper rest for American truckers.

"This question is being framed around how much the proposed rule, which limits the number of hours commercial truck drivers can be on the road, could cost consumers,"

Kucinich said, "But I would respectfully submit there are far more appropriate questions: whether this proposed rule will help ensure that all of our loved ones will be safe and able to enjoy each other's company, which the proposed rule, that is what it's all about, is saving lives."

Kucinich was ostensibly talking about the father and son seated just two rows behind the panel. Ed Slattery felt he was an audience of one as the congressman spoke. He traveled with Matthew from Baltimore to be in the hearing room. It felt good to be recognized and Ed was so incredibly hopeful that he and Matthew's presence was going to make a difference. Ed was not only representing himself, but he was looking to carry the load for the Truck Safety Coalition. He wanted his story to be heard from his lips, because he figured if those lawmakers heard about the last year of his life, they would certainly realize the economics of pain and loss.

Representative Dennis Kucinich certainly thought so. He explained to the panel that truck driver fatigue was a serious problem and threatens everyone who gets on a highway every day. The lawmaker made sure everyone in the room heard the number; 3,500 people killed, and 100,000 people injured in truck crashes each year, and one of them was sitting in the room.

"There are brave people in the audience today who came to support stricter standards for truck drivers, because they've been unfortunate to have felt firsthand the devastating effects of truck driver fatigue," Kucinich said, as he looked up from his prepared statement to make eye contact with Ed and Matthew in the audience.

The congressman made note of a statement Ed wrote to be put into the record, but then continued to read parts of it. Kucinich said he wanted the panel to understand the real cost of tired truckers and began reading excerpts without objection.

"It was a beautiful, clear day on August 16, 2010, when my family's lives were changed forever," Kucinich read. Sitting in the audience, Ed's eyes were fixed on the congressman's eyes darting back and forth across the paper, but, in his mind, he was silently recalling what he wrote, unconsciously tracing his own words under his breath. "My wife, Susan, and our two sons, Peter and Matthew were returning home from a big family reunion in Rocky River, Ohio," Kucinich read before pausing to say, "that happens to be in my district."

The Ohio representative continued to read parts of the Slattery story, including the death of Susan, the critical injuries to Peter and Matthew, and the fight to heal physically and emotionally. It was sincere, but being read into the record by a United States congressman, Ed couldn't help but feel his story reeked of apathy and sterility; it didn't land, he thought, and it didn't feel like a life altering moment. It felt like a formality.

Finally, Kucinich read the last part of Ed's statement, urging the subcommittee not to get in the way of a regulation he was convinced would save the lives of others. This last part was Ed's big finish. In so many ways, it reflected the maturation of all his pain, Matthew's suffering, and the family's loss. It was to be Ed's sobering warning he thought would trump all economic concerns, and this was the moment his pain would begin to have a purpose.

"Our lives will never be the same," Kucinich read, "but I can work to reduce truck driver fatigue so that another family will not have to suffer the tremendous loss that my family lives with every single day. If adopted, a proposed rule will save lives, improve driver health, reduce costs to society. I urge this subcommittee not to impede the progress the Department of Transportation has made to improve the HOS rule and protect the safety and well-being of our families." As Kucinich finished, he, again, looked up to find at Ed and Matthew in the audience. Ed stared back, proud of what he had written, and grateful the world had just heard it. Kucinich then spoke directly to Ed from the raised dais, "I just want you to know that we are going to be very sensitive to the concerns that are expressed here, and we thank you very much for attending this hearing, so that you can listen to the testimony."

Listen he did.

Chairman Jim Jordan then introduced the experts Republican leadership invited to discuss the proposed hours of service rule change, and from where Ed Slattery was sitting, the deck was stacked against the message he traveled with his disabled son from Baltimore to Capitol Hill to deliver.

Six men were sworn in to testify, starting with Mr. Ed Nagle, President and CEO of Nagle Companies, a transport company located just outside Jordan's congressional district. Jordan introduced Nagle with a warm, familiar smile before going down the row of witnesses that included more executive directors and CEOs of transportation companies, providers of various goods, and an economics firm, ready to testify just how much this new rule could cost everyone.

There was only one person representing people like Ed Slattery; just one, Henry Jasny, the Vice President of Advocates for Highway and Auto Safety. The rest would testify to how and why the proposed rule would cripple the trucking industry and end up costing Americans much more in the long run.

First up to make that point was Ed Nagle, who described the rich family tradition that led him to grow up in and pursue a successful career in the trucking industry. Nagle Companies started with his grandfather after World War II, he told the panel, and now served the top ten foods manufactures and distributors in the country. If the Department of Transportation reduced drive time by one hour and enforced the 34-hour restart provision, then his company's revenue opportunity would drop by 17%, he testified. To make up for that, he told his neighboring congressman, he would have to raise his rates by about 20%. Nagle continued to make his case, saying there was no need for the rule, that since 2003 there was a 33% drop in truck related fatalities as well as a 40% drop in truck-related injuries. But it was not just on a percentage basis Nagle continued, "On a per million-mile-basis has been significantly reduced."

Ed followed the argument Nagle was making. Intellectually, he understood the cost of Nagle to do business, and the facts he recited to convince the subcommittee to block the proposed rule, but it was the method he used to do it that infuriated Ed Slattery, to the point where he could sit and listen no more.

Ed felt Nagle was normalizing the data, making it standard. Instead of saying 3,500 people die each year in crashes with commercial motor vehicles, Nagle was taking that number and dividing it by millions of miles traveled. A neat little way of packaging a statistic to make it more easily digestible when it comes to real people killed on American roadways. Ed knew exactly how Nagle was dancing with numbers, except they were also lives. Ed grew angry, because he thought Nagle was trivializing the victims of tired truckers.

Ed remained calm about it, but no longer had respect for the partisan theater making a mockery of life and death. He rose from the audience and grabbed Matthew's wheelchair. There was no way to exit gracefully, but Ed almost preferred it that way. He and his son burst through the doors of the hearing room and into the marble hallway of the Rayburn House Office Building. It was there where his frustrations bubbled over to anyone who would listen.

"If this is what a Congressional hearing is like, then I understand why communism has a higher approval rating than Congress," he said in a frustrated tone that echoed through the halls. Ed didn't care who heard him, or that strangers began to take notice of the scene he was subconsciously trying to create. He simply couldn't bear the thought of his wife's life or his son's injuries being standardized away beneath the millions of wheels and countless miles of the trucking industry. His family, his life, was not to be treated like a widget, and the trucking industry shouldn't be maximizing its efficiency on stories like his.

The majority party gets to choose most of who speaks at congressional hearings. It is House rules. Ed knew that, but he had gone to Washington hoping to be heard rather than just read, especially if no one was going to counter the testimony of five straight pro-trucking interests.

"This whole hearing was a farce," Ed continued in the hallway. Only the caretaker he hired to help with Matthew and fellow advocates were around to hear him, but he was still loud enough to continue grabbing the attention of staffers walking through the cavernous hallways. "If the American people knew what these hearings were, I think they would be even more sickened than they are now."

To blow off some steam, Ed started to walk the hallways wheeling Matthew up and down. It worked, Ed calmed down and gained his composure just in time to see Chairman Jim Jordan exiting out the back door of the chamber to the public restroom around the corner.

Ed walked right up to the congressman just before he went into the bathroom and calmly and respectfully introduced himself.

"Sir, my name is Ed," he said extending his hand, "Congressman Kucinich read my statement into the record."

Representative Jordan was very apologetic and sympathetic, as he engaged in small talk Ed felt only facilitated a graceful exit from what was an uncomfortable interaction.

"Where are you going?" Ed asked.

The congressman replied and gestured toward the door both men were standing near, "The restroom."

"Well, with all due respect congressman, you should have a urinal under the desk and you should pee while you're doing your job, because that is what truckers have to do."

Jim Jordan's aide jumped in handing Ed Slattery his card, while the lawmaker ducked into the bathroom. The aide explained to Ed that any time he was in D.C., Jordan's office would arrange a meeting with anyone he wanted. But Ed wanted to speak with someone right then and there, and as the hearing ended and people spilled out into the hallway, he had his chance.

After a few choice words with associations and those representing the interests of the trucking industry, Ed cornered Congressman Dennis Kucinich.

"That was a farce," Ed said sternly, as if he was lecturing a class that just didn't understand his lesson on economics that day, "The rules of the House need to be changed. It is nuts to have all those people from the trucking interest lined up and only one safety advocate. Mr. Jordan knew what he believed when he walked in there, and everybody simply parroted what he wanted to hear."

The congressman from Susan's home district lent a sympathetic ear, knowing Ed's frustration wasn't directed at him, but seemed kind enough to be the sounding board.

"The important thing about Congress you have to remember," Kucinich told Ed, after he had expended his passionate plea, "even if you walk into a situation where the deck is stacked against you, if you can still get your point across. That is huge."

Even without a microphone or a seat at the table, Ed did get his point across to at least the audience in that hearing room that were now in the hallway. As Ed approached the decidedly pro trucking crowd, no one dared stop the poignant and emotionally heavy prose of a frustrated widower; not the chair of the subcommittee, not other lawmakers, and not even those lobbying for the trucking industry. All of them listened and didn't dare counter Ed's argument with the talking points the rule's opposition was ready to use to serenade the media. Ed didn't hear anyone say that decreased drive times could increase the cost of cereal, gas, clothing, or anything else Americans want to buy, or that fatigue isn't a leading reason crashes happen.

Ed knew members of the American Trucking Associations and other industry interests wouldn't dare hurl those refrains in his face in the halls of the Rayburn building after the hearing concluded. If not out of empathy, then politeness, the opposition was captive to Ed's hurt, pain, and most of all, an economics lesson he so desperately wanted to teach right there in the hallway.

"There are 330 million of us that can share that cost," Ed nearly shouted at the group huddled just a few yards away from him and his family. "As it stands right now, 3,000 families a year lose a family member and those 3,000 families bear that whole cost!"

Less than a month after the hearing, Transportation Secretary Ray LaHood announced the contested rule change. The hours of service for many truckers were cut from 82 to 70, and there would be a mandatory 34-hour restart time with two periods of sleep being between 1 a.m. and 5 a.m.; however, the 11-hour drive time limit per shift stayed intact and did not decrease.

Safety advocates applauded the Obama Administration for heeding the data of fatigue experts to create safer roads, but were disappointed with the unchanged drive time limits. Still, safety groups were convinced it would make for safer roads. The trucking industry, while grateful drive times were not decreased to ten hours, would live to fight the rest of the rule change before it was set to go into effect in July of 2013.

For Ed Slattery, he was pleased something was accomplished and that his story may have helped in some small way.

Nov 30, 2011 8:23pm
Dear Susan,

Well it was a long day and our little boy was quite the trooper. I think I am done parading him before the public. He needs to focus on being an adolescent boy who needs lots of rehab. I can fight the fight on my own from here on out. I know he's the 'star' but everyone will just have to live with looking at and hearing from me.

I think I did well in the press conference, but not so well in the hearing. I left the hearing after listening to industry advocates tell the committee for the fourth time in twenty minutes that the fatality rate has declined over the past several years. They are proud of only killing 3,000 people and not 4,000. Well, projections for this year are up over 4,000 again, and the committee chair said 'those are just projections'. As if they are going to be wildly off. Well, statisticians put those projections together, and this late in the year, they tend to be pretty good.

The selfishness of the industry advocates was palpable and unabashed. All they could talk about were increased costs to them. They even said, themselves, that they'd have to pass those costs off on to their customers. Well, I say that's fair.

The market price of all goods should reflect their true, total costs of production, including externalities such as pollution, health damages, lives lost, or bodies maimed. As it is, the trucking industry doesn't have to pay for the damages they cause. You did. We do. More than 13,000 individual drivers and their friends and families do.

All I ask is that the costs of safety be internalized by the trucking industry. If they pay for safety features that prevent deaths and injuries, and those costs are properly reflected in the prices of their products, then we will have achieved something. That's econ 101. It's not liberal or conservative, Catholic or Protestant, Islamic or Jewish, black, white, or other. It's safety, pure and simple. Don't make it any more complicated than that.

I hope you are proud.

We love and miss you,

Ed

Chapter 12

Decamber in Maryland can have a no-going-back kind of feel. The trees are finally bare, their branches and bark seem brittle, and the air is cold, tight, and dry. Winter can settle in slowly in the mid-Atlantic, but there comes a time of year where the sky becomes set in its ways like an old man finally comfortable with being in the rear view of modern American life.

It was on one of autumn's swan song days when Ed Slattery received a letter from the Portage County Prosecutor's Office. Doug Bouch was set for sentencing in Susan's death, and Peter and Matthew's injuries. Ed was invited to attend and provide a victim impact statement. It could be written, recorded, or he could attend the hearing in person and read what he had to say into the record himself. He could look Doug Bouch in the eye for the first time.

It was an opportunity Ed could not pass up. It would have been easier to send a letter but he wanted to see the man who killed his wife and have him listen to why she mattered, why Matthew and Peter matter, and why the life he once knew mattered.

Ed took weeks to carefully craft his statement. It was, after all, the culmination of a year and a half of pain, grief, and struggle. Choosing what to say, what not to say, and how to express all of it was a heavy burden. There would be other statements, but Ed's would be the keynote address.

It all had to matter, and he would waste no words on a sermon or emotion or hyperbole. The statement had to strike the right balance for the judge, defendant, and victim to truly echo the love and loss of nearly two years.

It took weeks. Ed tweaked it several times before making the trip in mid-January to see what fate had in store for the man who killed Susan.

Shortly after the second Christmas without Susan, Ed chose to drive out to Ravenna, Ohio with his daughter, Kelli. He made the decision not to bring Matthew or Peter. Peter simply wanted nothing to do with it, and Ed thought Matthew wouldn't understand the proceeding. It was not worth the emotion of either of his sons to litigate the decisions that forever changed their lives. This was Ed's cross to bear, and he was as prepared as he was going to be to carry it past the television news cameras and into the courtroom.

There, Ed, Kelli, and Susan's family sat as Judge John Enlow called case number 2011 CR 00483, State of Ohio versus Douglas Bouch. Doug and his attorney Errol Can sat at a table in front of the bench. Their backs were to the gallery, leaving Ed to still wonder what Doug Bouch looked like. Instead, Ed studied his back, his movements, and the occasional profile, as he leaned in to whisper to his attorney.

A courtroom is where some of the richest human emotions are spent. The anticipation of them in such close quarters only serves to thicken moods and amplify nervous whispering chatter. The gavel slamming on the wooden bench is the only sound that can pierce the tension with its jarring clarity and, perhaps, inevitability. As Judge Enlow's gavel fell, the courtroom snapped to attention; a clatter followed by silent anticipation.

"Mr. Can, do you wish to offer any evidence?" the judge asked from his bench.

"Your Honor, I wish to make a brief statement, and, if my client is capable, he may, also."

"All right," the judge said, "You may proceed."

"Thank you, Your Honor. May it please the Court? Your Honor, I will be brief here. And I think that I probably ought to start off by saying that every comment that I'm going to make here in the next couple of minutes is with the understanding that whenever, whatever I say about Doug, and the sentencing guidelines, and this case, and whatever affect it had on Doug, and his life, and his family, pales in comparison to the Slattery family, so I hope that all comments I make are taken in that vein, Your Honor."

It was the right thing to say. Ed quietly acknowledged that much. After all, this wasn't about revenge. Ed wasn't wired in that eye-for-an eye kind of way. As much pain as his family was forced to feel from all this, he was actually sympathetic to Doug Bouch's plight. Ed wasn't a man of great means, at least not as he lived life prior to this crash, but he was an educated man, and one who knew Bouch was a victim of the same industry. The circumstances were greatly different, but the root cause was the same. It was something Ed innately understood, but not all pain in that courtroom was created equal.

"Your Honor," Can continued, "In looking at the sentencing guidelines here, let me start off by mentioning that Doug walked in here and pled [sic] to this. He did not want to put this family through any more than they've, God knows, already been through. This was a horrible, horrible tragedy.

"As you can see, Your Honor... this is the type of case where there was no intent on Doug's part to harm anybody. He's lived a law-abiding life his entire life. He's a father, husband, a grandfather. The only thing that has sustained him through this is family...church, his faith. Your Honor, with regard to Chapter 2929 of the Ohio Revised code, I think that we always look at the term 'genuine remorse' and throw that around...In Doug's case, Your Honor, he's done everything he can. You can't turn back the clock. He's done whatever he could, in terms of the civil case, cooperating without going to trial, pleading to this right off the bat, doing everything he can to try to make things a little bit easier for the family, and I hope it maybe made it a little bit easier. God knows, he prays for them every day. His family prays for them every day."

Ed quietly listened. He remained stoic and consciously tried to show no emotion. He wanted to see the remorse from Doug Bouch.

"Your Honor, genuine remorse is an understatement here," Can continued, "He lives with this every day. And, again, take this in the vein that what he's going through does pale in comparison to the Slattery family, but, nevertheless, there's not a moment that he doesn't realize that he was at fault, that he created this incredibly horrible tragedy. He's going to have to carry on for his family. It's very difficult. He's in a trade school to learn electronics, so that he can get back to work and support his family.

"When we look at the overriding principles of the felony sentencing guidelines in this case, Your Honor, clearly, in reviewing the presentence investigation and just the nature of this case, and that there was no intent to harm anyone, his punishment is having to live with this for the rest of his life and know that his actions brought about this horrible tragedy on this wonderful family. To incarcerate him, Your Honor, under the sentencing guidelines, what are we protecting the public from? This man is not a danger to the public whatsoever. He's led a law-abiding life. He's a family man, a church-going man."

Ed fidgeted in his seat. He was growing impatient with the prayers and God-driven excuses Bouch's lawyer kept serving up to the judge. From where Ed sat, all he could see was the backs of lawyer and client, but did have a clear view of Judge Enlow's face. He studied it, as he could sense Can wrapping up. Ed wanted to see if the judge was buying what he found to be increasingly hollow and patronizing.

"The fact of the matter is, he's cooperated entirely from the moment the accident happened. As a matter of fact, if he probably hadn't spoken with the highway patrol, I'm not so sure this indictment could have come down this way. But he was truthful with the officers, told them everything he could think of, and, from day one, he has tried to do right by the Slattery family, Your Honor."

And so what? Ed thought, if not for Doug Bouch being honest, this whole thing would have washed away on a technicality? The mere implication that Bouch doing the right thing was enough to mention in a court of law began to anger Ed. He got it; Doug Bouch wasn't a highly educated man and was the bluest of blue collar living his honest life on a farm, but just because he told the truth did not erase the responsibility he must own in killing Susan. Ed's brow began to furrow as he contemplated the narrative of the selfless truck driver.

"With that, Your Honor, I would indicate that to grant community control, certainly, would not demean the seriousness of the offense. Now, clearly, when I say the seriousness of the offense, I'm really pointing out the fact that there was no intent to harm anyone…just a horrible tragedy…and he certainly does not need to be incarcerated to protect the family, Your Honor. Thank you."

Errol Can sat back down next to his client. While perhaps not delivered eloquently, he made some valid points. Doug Bouch wasn't a violent man and did not need to be incarcerated for what was a grave mistake, but whether or not he meant to commit the crime was irrelevant in the court of law and to Ed.

"Thank you, Your Honor. At this time, the State has two victim impact statements; Ed Slattery and his sister-in-law," the prosecutor said.

As Susan's older sister Thea made her way up to the podium to read her statement, Ed remained seated in the gallery. He was half-paying attention to Thea. He knew what she would say, hell he knew the woman she was talking about better than most in the room. Susan was energetic, a committed educator, and a loving sister, Thea would tell the court. She absolutely resented having to see her elderly parents deal with the loss of their second child.

Ed listened, but was more focused on the man with his back to him. While the podium didn't face where Doug Bouch was seated in the courtroom, he noticed the man never turned his head to see the pain in Thea's eyes, as she read into the record what an absolute "dynamo" her younger sister was. Doug Bouch's mere profile irked Ed. He felt Bouch should have to meet his eyes, so he didn't miss any of the words he or Susan's family wrote with their tears.

Ed sat in the court gallery knowing he was up next, but just couldn't shake the idea that Bouch was just passively or, at best, defensively listening to the pain he had caused. *And why?* Ed thought to himself. *Because he didn't mean to? Well he should have a better fucking excuse than that of a child spilling a drink at the dinner table.*

Ed began to feel himself building a diatribe in his mind when he heard Thea wrap up her statement.

"The impact of the loss of our beloved Susan will be felt for the rest of our lives. Thank you," Thea said, as she backed away from the podium.

Ed hugged Thea and then walked up to the podium himself. He laid his statement down and prepared to read the measured words he spent weeks crafting. He glanced to his right to see just a profile of Doug Bouch. He was even with him now, no longer just staring at his back, but far from looking into the man's eyes. Ed felt cheated. He felt the words he was about to say were going to be peripherally comprehended, and it angered him even more. Susan Slattery's life, Matthew's injuries, and the decisions Doug Bouch made that summer morning were not to be reduced to the disembodied text in the court reporter's eventual transcription. Doug Bouch may not have been looking at Ed Slattery, but he most certainly would have to listen to what Ed was about to say, all of it from the heart, but the first few from the gut.

"Your Honor, my name is Ed Slattery. I come to you today as a widower. I want to make one brief comment about Mr. Bouch's lawyer's comments."

Ed was off script. His original words were printed and in front of him. At any point, he could look down and begin to read off the measured, calculated brew he had stewed over the last few weeks. Those words were important; they were what needed to be said and they would, but not before a brief rebuttal to Bouch's attorney. And if Bouch wasn't going to look at him then he would speak these words directly to Judge Enlow.

"On the issue of intent, Your Honor. I've always raised my children, when they were two and three years old and spilled their milk, and they would say 'I'm sorry' – and I know they meant it, in their two and three year old way – but I always told them, that's fine, but we have to fix it. We would fix it. We would clean it up and it would be over. I never wanted them to live with that spilled milk. They fixed it. And I think that's what my religious upbringing teaches me, is to fix it. Then they would say, 'I didn't mean to,' when they got a bit older, and I would say, well, whether you meant it or not doesn't matter. It happened. What are you going to do? And these are the exact words I would say, 'What are you going to do, someday, when you're driving on the road and you didn't mean to kill somebody, but you did? I can't fix that.'"

Ed sounded almost surprised at the irony as the words came out of his mouth. The lesson he used to teach his children as toddlers literally played out in schooling the forty-nine-year-old man who killed their mother.

"So, intent," Ed said gathering himself as he looked over at Doug Bouch, who still didn't have the nerve or respect to look at him, "I'm sure Mr. Bouch did not intend to do this, but it happened." Ed paused. He wanted the weight, the irony, and the figurative and literal meanings of what he just said to collide as forcefully as they just did in his head. He wanted the judge and the courtroom to savor that point before looking down at his prepared words.

"So, I'd like to say now this is my statement: I am not here to avenge Susan's death or the permanent damage to my sons, myself, Susan's two step-children, her two parents, five siblings, twenty-three nieces and nephews, and numerous friends, students, and countless colleagues. I am here to eke out whatever justice can be eked out of this tragedy.

"I don't know about sentencing guidelines. I do know about fairness. I, actually, am a Ph.D., an economist, and I teach fairness and different concepts of fairness. Mr. Bouch made some very bad choices on the days leading up to the crash, and he needs to suffer some of the consequences beyond the personal suffering, which I think he feels in his heart, and I do think he needs to spend a little bit of time in jail.

"Susan was a department head of mathematics. She was a female with a Ph.D. in mathematics. She developed girls and minorities in science and math for the entire life of our marriage.

"She worked with our boys' classes, since they were in preschool, on science and math. She did field trips, robot clubs, and special activities affecting countless other children. She helped build science labs in our small Catholic School. She was a den mother in Cub Scouts for both of our boys. She had just taken over a major fund-raiser before she was killed.

"She helped raise hundreds of thousands of dollars for various schools and organizations over the past eighteen years, and never accepted a dime or a 'thanks.' She didn't want thanks; she just wanted to do what needed to be done.

"She was a beloved teacher and administrator on track to becoming a dean, or more, at a university in the United States when she was killed."

Ed flipped the page at the podium as if to turn to the next chapter in his ongoing tragedy from Susan's death to Matthew. Poised to hold up a picture of Matthew in his hospital bed the first night after the crash, Ed began to tell the judge just who his son was, and now is.

"Matthew was a normal, active, animated, loving 12-year-old the day he was maimed by Mr. Bouch. This is what I saw when I arrived at the hospital that day, twelve hours after hearing what happened, because that's how long it took me to get to them. Mr. Bouch took not only his mother, but his future. The little boy I saw in the hospital that day was hardly recognizable. He was alive by the grace of God, in the able hands of doctors, nurses, and one of his rescuers, who is here today. It was not clear that he was going to survive that month in Akron.

"Taking care of and worrying about Matthew, I haven't gotten to mourn the loss of my wife.

"Matthew spent time in the hospital in Akron. He spent one week in John Hopkins and five months in-patient at Kennedy Krieger Institute in Baltimore. His head was bent to the right, and his arm and leg were curled and immobile. He was still not fully conscious after nearly six months.

"Matthew then did nine months of intense therapy five days a week, six hours a day. Imagine being in a gym six hours a day, Your Honor. During that time, he's learned to talk a little bit, walk 100 feet with a walker, with assistance, roll over on a mat, eat by himself and finally, he can use a toilet for bowel movements; although, the other night, I had to digitally stimulate his rectum to help him move his bowels, which was very painful. He still cannot urinate on his own, and we catheterize him every six hours. He's in Kennedy Krieger for developmentally disabled children. While adjusting, he doesn't understand why he isn't at his old school with his old friends. I'm not even sure he understands his mother is dead. Mr. Bouch took away our ability to communicate with Matthew. He has aphasia, something suffered when you have a stroke.

"He can't read or write, and this is particularly upsetting, because he was a voracious reader. He doesn't even like for us to read to him today, because he can't keep up.

"Peter was sixteen at the time. He was the lucky one, because he only suffered a crushed pelvis and broken eye orbit. He was conscious though, and kind of knew what was going on, and I'm thankful for his rescuer, who removed him from the scene as quickly as possible. He saw his brother in a coma. He was told that his mother died in the crash. He was drugged and confused and got several infections and had to go under the knife three times. And, just two months ago, he had a stitch removed that was embedded in his hip. He can no longer play rugby, and I worry about what the long-running effects will be when he's our age.

"As close as he and I are, we go camping together every month, where he mostly ignores me. I can't imagine what it is like to lose your mother and brother, and survive for a 16-year-old. What is he doing with the survivor guilt? Does he have any? What does it mean to lose your homegrown math tutor when you're taking trig and calculus? My 16-year-old says, 'I just can't do anything about Mom and Matthew, so why lie around and wallow?' Does he understand it's normal and okay to wallow? Will this haunt him in ten, twenty, thirty years? What kind of person, spouse, parent is he going to be as a result of losing his mother and brother? Does he know how little of my time he gets because of his brother's recovery? I don't know. As a father I have to think about all these things. He doesn't, because he doesn't know any better. But I do.

"What about me? Well, I lost the love of my life; my partner, my friend. But I haven't had any time to even mourn her death, because I spend so much time with the boys. I've had to resign my position as an economist at USDA; fifty-five-years-old, retired, losing experience and years of service. What's it going to be like finding a job in a couple years when Matthew has, hopefully, recovered enough to allow me to work? We had to move from our inaccessible apartment to a much more expensive house. Nothing in my life is the same. I sit and lie in the living room and can't even fantasize my wife walking across it, because she never has.

"What about Susan's parents and siblings, this most wonderful family that I married into? Can you imagine losing your youngest child and sibling, the one who should have out-lived everyone? Our nieces and nephews have lost her, just as our children have. Mr. Bouch stole from our family the one person who called every one of them every weekend. And she was one of seven. There are six surviving siblings that she called every weekend. Susan was the one who sent care packages to our college freshman nieces and nephews during first years of final exams, cards and gifts to her Godchildren every year. Mr. Bouch stole a life force.

"Susan would sit in a chair at 10:00 at night with a cup of black coffee in her hand and fall asleep drinking coffee. She was exhausted.

"I don't seek revenge from Mr. Bouch. It doesn't do anybody any good. I do, however, seek justice. There are three reasons for sentencing Mr. Bouch to serve some prison time; the first is as retribution for the damage he caused by irresponsible actions. And the fact that 'I didn't mean to' doesn't change anything. I'm not really interested in retribution so much. I'm not angry for that. I do have forgiveness in my heart, and, Your Honor, I'm a bleeding heart liberal. We believe people should take responsibility for their actions.

"The second is to prevent Mr. Bouch from reoffending. I'm somewhat interested in that, but do not believe Mr. Bouch is inclined to ever drive a truck again, and would hope that the state wouldn't allow it. Anyway, from what my attorneys tell me, there may not be any way to really prevent it.

"The third is deterrent to other truckers, and here's where I may come into conflict with your sentencing guidelines, but I believe, Your Honor, that you have an opportunity today to send a message to truckers throughout this country.

"Commercial truckers are involved in accidents that cause over 3,500 deaths every year. That's 9/11 every year. The airline industry would not get away with this. Amtrak would not get away with this. How is it that the trucking industry does? I have answers to that, but that's not of any interest here. Clearly, not all these accidents are the trucker's fault.

"I'm not here to say that truckers are bad people, or that Mr. Bouch is a bad person, but when you drive a truck, you are different than everybody else; you have to be better than everybody else. A surgeon has to be better than everybody else, because you chose to be that person, to take on that responsibility. Commercial truck drivers cannot rush to get somewhere, they can't get angry because of some irresponsible passenger vehicle next to them, and God knows they are meant to be plenty rested and inspect their vehicles for defects before they drive. Just as motorists, boats, and cars must give way to pedestrians, they must give way to passenger vehicles. It is unacceptable for them to drive tired, especially when they had several days off in which to get rested.

"Your Honor, Mr. Bouch deserves, and I believe needs, to do some time, to do penance, and to think about what he's done without the comfort of his family and — it's somewhat of a Buddhist perspective, perhaps — to sit and contemplate without the distractions, even of the ones that you love. But — and I don't care if this violates your sentencing — to set a good example to an industry and individual drivers that bad decisions lead to bad consequences, and the only way to stop this kind of death and savagery, and tens of thousands of people who are injured by truck drivers, like my sons, is to set a clear example.

"Ohio is one of the few states in the country that allows triple tractor trailers on its highway, and they restrict them to the right lane, because they're so unsafe. My question is, if they're that damn unsafe, why are they on the highway at all? They're not allowed to change lanes. I drive the interstate, too, and I see them changing lanes all the time with no consequences.

"Laws that have no consequences are meaningless. Meaningless. And we actually study that in economics. You can have the death penalty for jaywalking; if you never enforce it, it doesn't matter.

"I'm sorry, Mr. Bouch. I truly am. And I'm sorry for the position that I have to take, but I have to take it, because I think it's the responsible position. I am happy to meet with Mr. Bouch at any time, so that we can talk and that we can heal. I would even enlist Mr. Bouch to help us do some promotional material that might prevent this from happening to other people and other truckers. They are honorable people, they do honorable work, but they need to do it honorably. Thank you."

Ed finished his prepared statement at the podium and glanced over at the table to see if Doug Bouch was looking back. He wasn't. Still, Ed stood there and studied his profile. It was the most he had seen of the man who caused his life to irrevocably change, and he wasn't that impressed. Bouch wasn't as tall as Ed, and seemed in average shape with an average short haircut. Ed didn't know what to expect. Maybe, in his subconscious, he expected more dramatic features, but Bouch was unremarkable; an everyday guy you wouldn't notice in a crowd. In Ed's mind's eye all this time, he just thought the man responsible for the extraordinary wouldn't appear so...ordinary.

Ed turned and took his seat. He didn't know what was next or where the proceeding would go, but he said the piece he traveled all the way from Baltimore to say and, at the very least, he knew Bouch heard him.

"Mr. Finnegan," the judge said, as Ed began to take his seat.

The state prosecutor rose to address the judge and wrap his case. Ed would be the last bit of emotion the court would hear, but the prosecutor added the postscript to argue for what the state of Ohio thought was the appropriate punishment for Doug Bouch.

"Your Honor, I've had a lot of time to speak with Mr. Slattery over the last few months...and the way he sums it up best is, he's not a vengeful person, but he's a true believer that there is a justice system, and at this point it's the State's belief that...the Court is going to sentence in the manner most appropriate, certainly, but the one interesting point is that this wasn't a bad lane change. This wasn't a, you know, five-miles-over-the-speed-limit-on-an-entry-ramp kind of thing. This is what the indictment says. *It was reckless.* It was due to his carelessness and recklessness that ultimately caused the death of Susan Slattery and the injuries to her two sons. Quite frankly, it's amazing that, as devastating as this was, that more wasn't done, and I think it's just important to realize that, you know, as a truck driver, he does have a great responsibility. And, while in speaking with Mr. Can, we certainly are in agreement that he's not going to drive a truck ever again, and both parties are willing to put that in the record. That's one of the conditions we spoke about; he's never going to apply for a CDL, or become a truck driver in any fashion, [but] at that time; however, he was a truck driver and did have a responsibility to control his vehicle in a manner a lot better than what he did.

"Based upon that, Your Honor, we'd ask the Court to sentence as it deems appropriate under these very tragic circumstances."

The prosecutor thanked the court and sat back down. The room grew quiet again, with only the ambient sound of papers shuffling and the low hum of the heated air circulating the thick anticipation and anxiety throughout the room.

"Mr. Bouch?" Judge Enlow said breaking the silence.

"Can I address the family, please?" Bouch asked.

"Absolutely."

Ed sat up. It was the first time he heard the man's voice.

Bouch stood up and began to address the judge, his back still to Ed and Susan's family.

"Sir, I can't comprehend what that family is going through, and I don't have the words to convey how, not sorry, but sorrowful – if that's a word — that I am."

Bouch struggled to express himself, as he was literally at the mercy of the court.

"If it's any consequence, whatsoever, to them, despite of a whole lot of things that were reported about, there was nothing that I could have done differently to change that, and if I could, I would. If I could, in any way, change places with their family member that they lost, I sincerely and gladly would do that.

"I have gotten out of the truck, and I'm back in school full time. I never wanted to take an opportunity to have that happen again. I would be more than happy to help them in any way I can. I took the plea, I've done everything within my limited power in all of this to make it as easy for them as possible. And I don't mean to minimalize [sic] it, but I'm sorry. It wasn't a matter of, I didn't mean to. That's not it. There was no 'mean to' or anything to it. It was unavoidable. I cannot..."

Bouch broke down. He could not recover.

"I'm done, sir."

Ed watched Bouch sit back down. Not once did Bouch turn around and actually address Ed or Susan's family. He was pleading for the mercy of the court and merely spoke about the lives his actions affected as the tragic means to his end. It all seemed fairly selfish to Ed. He was disappointed Bouch never turned around or made a personal plea of forgiveness, but to tell the judge there was nothing he could have done, that it was all unavoidable...that sentiment was infuriating. Ed didn't accept that the accident was unavoidable, and neither did the state of Ohio.

"These cases are tragedies for two families," Judge Enlow said, "I feel for both of you. However, the Court, upon considering all the factors, makes the following findings:

"That at least two of the multiple offenses were committed as part of one or more courses of conduct, and the harm caused by those two or more of the multiple offenses committed was so great, or unusual, that no single prison term for any of the offenses committed as part of that conduct adequately reflects the seriousness of the offender's conduct. Based on that, it will be the sentence of this Court, on Count One, aggravated vehicular homicide, that you be confined by the Ohio Department of Corrections for a period of three years.

"On Count Two, vehicular assault, you shall be confined by the Ohio Department of Corrections for a period of one year.

"On Count Three, vehicular assault, that you be confined by the Ohio Department of Corrections for a period of one year. They are all to run consecutive to each other."

Five years.

Ed was shocked, dumbfounded. Five years was a stiff penalty and, as he watched Doug being taken into custody of the sheriff, Ed actually felt badly for the man.

Justice may be blind, but she forces nearly every other sense to respond when she balances her scale on personal tragedy.

Ed, Kelli, and Susan's family made their way out of the courtroom and into the lobby, filled with a bank of local news cameras and print reporters looking for his reaction. Truth was, he didn't know what his reaction was going to be until he began to speak into microphones.

Ed explained how he was shocked and expected Bouch to only get probation. At best he thought maybe one or two years in prison. Five years was a statement. It was one Ed hoped the court would make about the trucking industry, but now saw it was at the expense of another life and another family. He explained to the media how he would support an early release date and hoped maybe, one day, he and Bouch could meet again; maybe they could work together on a public awareness campaign on trucker safety.

"I think it will help him heal," Ed was quoted in the local newspaper, "And I think it will help me heal."

Dear Susan,

So while we are pleased that the judge sent a clear message to truckers across the country, we are sickened that this man has to spend five years in jail. I seriously doubted that he'd spend any time in jail and am not sure that five years isn't too stiff.

I was pretty tough on him in my victim impact statement, which was, in reality, much tougher than what I posted earlier. My tone was tough and my words tougher still.

To what extent did my words add to his trouble? Jeff tells me to stay away from that question. Mr. Bouch is responsible for where he is and the judge handed down the sentence. I did not mention any specific jail term, that is true. So maybe my statement didn't make any difference with the judge.

I am not very coherent about this, because I am so unsure of my feelings. Just as Mr. Bouch has to live with his choices, I have to live with mine.

I love you, sweetheart, and we all miss you so much. Your family is reeling from your loss and will never be the same. However, we do laugh, and we do really appreciate each other, and are so grateful to have Peter and Matthew. Thank you for them.

Ed

Chapter 13

That was supposed to be the end.

After all, Ed Slattery won a near record breaking civil suit against the trucking company, and the judge in the criminal case flirted with records as well by handing down the strictest sentence to date for a trucker whose fatigue transformed his rig into a lethal weapon on an American interstate.

While the word *win* lacks the emotive properties behind the true end-result of tragedy, Ed Slattery earned a convincing judgment against the trucking industry, both civilly and criminally. In the annals of traditional journalistic storytelling, the sentencing of Doug Bouch marked closure. But for the Slatterys, closure was yet another one of those words that came up short on describing the intricacies of human suffering. Closure is overused and underserves victims of violent crime or immense trauma. There was no closure on January 12, 2012. The sentencing of Bouch only served to continue the tragic narrative writing itself in Ed Slattery's mind; a narrative he sat down to compose in a letter to the man who killed his wife less than one month after he was sent away for five years.

"Mr. Bouch," Ed began simply.

A proper greeting like 'Dear' just didn't seem appropriate. While Doug Bouch had five years, Ed wasn't looking to waste any time with contrived salutations.

> *I don't really know how to start this letter other than to say, 'I don't really know how to start this letter.'*
>
> *What I really want to say is that I am so full of sorrow for you and your family. I mean that. As rough as I was on you at the sentencing hearing, please understand that I was talking to the*

entire industry, not just you. It is unfortunate for both of us that we have to be examples for others, but here we are.

My wife's family was in the courtroom at the sentencing hearing, also, and I want you to know that we were all a bit surprised at how stiff the penalty was. It is not what we expected. Having said that, I think it sends the 'right' message to all truckers, and I hope we can get the word about this sentence out, as well as others, to the industry, so that we can stop the killing and maiming.

I also want you to know that, as angry as I am, I forgive you. It is not my place to judge you beyond your actions here on Earth. You are being held to account for them as determined by an earthly court. How you and God come to an understanding of this is between you two. I will have to deal with God on my own, but know that the first thing I have to do is forgive you.

I do!

I look forward to hearing from you in the near future. How can we reconcile between ourselves, and how can we make a positive difference in the world? We are inextricably bound now. Let's make something good out of it.

Sincerely,
Ed Slattery

For Ed Slattery, he hoped closure was to be found in a new relationship with the man convicted of taking his wife's life and his son's future. Ed wanted to marry his misfortunes with Doug Bouch's and for the two of them to transform their pain into making a difference. A long shot, sure. A big ask with even bigger odds, but it was truly the only way Ed saw purpose in the tragedy. He had truly hoped Bouch could feel the same and waited eagerly for a response.

As winter turned into spring, no letter arrived. While it certainly bothered Ed, he had no time for harboring resentment. Bouch was where he was and, as far as Ed was concerned, serving time for the grave mistake he made. Ed, while remaining curious of Bouch's reaction to his letter, had more important concerns that required his energy and focus. He needed to figure what was next for himself and his family. He needed to move forward by letting go.

There were no more courts, no more judges, lawyers, mediations or reporters. After a dizzying and life-altering year and a half, life got eerily quiet and still.

Ed realized he needed a blueprint for the next steps in his life and the lives of his family. It was on a hilltop in a suburb north of Baltimore where that vision struck him. Ed now had the financial means to move his family out of their standard split level rental and create a home free of the frustrations of the disabled living in an able bodied world.

Ed purchased a lot that overlooked the skyline of Towson, Maryland and interviewed architects and builders until he found the right combination. He was looking for an architect with no preconceived notions of what living with a disability was and a builder who would accept Ed's goals of extreme accessibility, sustainability, and his penchant for buying American-made products when possible. Most importantly, Ed needed his team to buy into what the house would be and, most importantly, for whom.

Ed found that in a small but innovative architecture firm in Baltimore called Alter Urban and builder Paul Lichter. "This isn't to be any old house for any old family; this is a special home for Matthew. A home Matthew could live in the rest of his life," Ed told the team.

It was a concept evident from design to build. The home was to be laid out in an L-shape and include mighty, dramatic arches tied into a more than 50-foot 22-inch thick cement wall buried into the side of a hill. The design relieved the need for load bearing walls on purpose. Ed saw what Matthew's wheelchair could do to walls and doors, and wanted to create a space where none of it was a factor. Remove the hurdles, Ed thought, and enable Matthew.

Ed needed a home that helped Matthew grow into his disability. While Matthew continued to improve through intensive physical and occupational therapy, and was just beginning to fall into a routine at a special school for the disabled, he was still a prisoner of his injuries because of his environment.

Matthew couldn't get to the other level of the current home, he didn't cook, and he couldn't get around without gouging a wall or a cabinet. The house Ed would help design and build eliminated all of it and, in turn, liberate Matthew and his self-esteem.

The floor would be finished concrete, the rugs sunk to meet at level so there wasn't a lip anywhere, thus creating a continuous surface. Most doors would be pocket doors and the baseboards 12" high. Wheelchair proof, Ed called it. The design also called for a therapy pool area, accessible showers and benches, pull down cabinets and cook tops, and even a power assisted pulley system to access a meditation tower offering a view of Towson, Maryland.

The state of the art home would be beyond the wildest dreams of the Americans with Disabilities Act pioneers. In addition, it would be sustainable. Geothermal energy would heat the four thousand square feet, and solar panels would power them. The roof was green with plants and herbs to be harvested for meals, and the driveway was made of porous asphalt to prevent any storm water runoff.

It was a $3 million design, but Ed wanted Matthew to never need anything the rest of his life. While money couldn't replace Susan, or the dexterity of his youngest son, it could certainly help.

The endgame from the very first drawings was to find the family's new normal. Normal, of course, is a relative term, and finding one's way back to his definition of it is often a journey to an entirely unexpected destination. Ed found himself defining it through the architects, who helped to create the space that wasn't normal for a regular residence, but would allow for Matthew, Peter, and Ed to resume their new definition of it.

The house would also honor Susan's memory. Within the design and along a concrete surface, Ed wanted to print the number and mathematical constant, Pi. He wanted it to continue for as long at the surface would allow, an ode to the mother of his children and the stability of the woman he would forever miss. For while she was gone, the love they had for her was as infinite as her favorite number.

With the blueprints set, models built, and sketches drawn, Ed's team broke ground as the weather got warmer. Ed would be involved in the project every day for the better part of two years, as designers and builders pieced together the life he architected for his family, ever moving forward, until a letter arrived in the mail from the Portage County Prosecutors Office.

The victims' assistance office notified Ed that Doug Bouch and his attorney filed a motion asking the judge to shorten his sentence. Bouch was four months into a five-year long sentence, and he was seeking relief.

"Now comes the defendant, through undersigned counsel, and respectfully requests that this Honorable Court reconsider the previously imposed sentence," the first line of the motion read.

Bouch's attorney Errol Can, citing a recently passed state law, argued his client should be eligible for a judicial release by July of 2012. Judicial release in Ohio law gives the sentencing judge the power and discretion to release an inmate from his or her sentence after a certain amount of time. In Bouch's case, he was eligible to apply after 180 days of incarceration.

The Ohio State House Bill 86, which was effective as of August 2011, could very well apply, but the evidence offered to argue such a release from prison was damn near offensive to the Slattery family.

Can argued in the motion that Ed Slattery wouldn't much mind Bouch's early release. "Defendant's attorney has cause to believe that the victims would not be opposed to such a reconsideration," the motion read. "To this point, a copy of a CaringBridge.org journal entry made by victims Peter and Matthew Slattery and an article from the January 13, 2012 edition of the Akron Beacon Journal are attached as Exhibit A."

Can attached a copy of what he thought was just a journal entry but, in effect, was Ed's conversation with his wife. It was on a public blog and fair game, but Can's brief lacked emotion. The attorney, in essence, bastardized Ed's words, intent and, worst of all, sensationalized a private but open letter to his dead wife; the woman his client killed.

For those who read the entries and letters to Susan considered them a privilege, a glimpse into the love and life of two souls. Ed was a man finding his way though immense trauma by talking out loud to the partner he lost. He was grieving in one to three Dear Susan's a day, and graciously allowed his friends and family to bear witness to it; not for a lawyer to use without his permission to free the man that took it all away from him.

Adding insult to all the injury was the other part of Can's exhibit, an article from the Akron Beacon Journal just after his client's sentencing. Buried in the story was a paraphrased quote from Ed expressing his shock at the five-year sentence and that he might be open to early release. But the article also had pictures showing the Slattery's return to Akron a year later to say thank you to the Akron Children's Hospital and first responders. The picture the editor chose to accompany the article was a high five between Ed and Matthew in Akron. Can's motion with the inclusion of the article along with Ed's intimate journal entry seemed to say to the judge, "See, this family is fine. They are healing okay, and even Ed thinks Doug Bouch should get out early."

Ed was confident Judge Enlow was going to see through the attempt at reducing Bouch's sentence. He was told in no uncertain terms that Can would be unsuccessful. Still, it only served to anger Ed, knowing the letter he wrote to Bouch had gone unanswered for months, a frustration he would make clear to the judge himself.

"Dear Judge Enlow, I am writing in reference to the hearing for Mr. Douglas Bouch and his appeal to reduce his sentence to less than five years," Ed began.

"I have discussed the general issue with my and Susan's family. There are two points of view. The first is that we don't care either way, as nothing will bring Susan back or return the boys to their full health, Matthew, in particular, being permanently disabled. The second is that we do not totally object to Mr. Bouch being able to *'earn'* early release; however, he has not made any effort to contact us to apologize for his actions."

Ed wanted the radio silence he received after being the better man and reaching out to Bouch behind bars to be clearly heard by the court.

"As I remember his statement in court, he said the accident couldn't be avoided," Ed continued, "If that is what he said, then he has not taken full responsibility for his actions, and we would be reluctant to see him released early. However, if he were to make a sincere apology and offer to help in some way to educate commercial vehicle drivers of their responsibilities on our highways, we would be more inclined to support his petition."

After Ed updated Judge Enlow on the condition of his children, he finished the letter by saying, "The loss of Susan is bad, but watching your children deal with that and their own physical deficits is even worse. I pray that Mr. Bouch never has to know how we feel."

And until he at least tried, Ed thought, fine then. Let him sit in jail, which the judge ultimately decided he would.

Chapter 14

*M*r. Slattery,

Please bear with me as I'm honestly not sure where to start. How does one even put into words all that needs to be said? How do I go about saying to you what's in my heart and on my mind without offending you or causing you further hurt? Please know in advance the sincerity with which this is written. It's not my intention to try to pacify you in any way, however, it is my intention in this letter to convey to you briefly how much my heart aches for you and your family.

It was a good start to a letter Ed felt was at best, a few months late. Well, a few months and two weeks. The letter with a return address of Lake Erie Correctional Institution sat sealed on his desk until he felt like he was prepared to read what Doug Bouch had to say.

When it felt right, Ed carefully opened the letter with the trepidation of a child watching a horror movie through their fingers. Ed gently flipped up the first fold, revealing what was inside the mind of the man who killed his wife. The letter was handwritten on two ruled pages ripped out from a legal pad. The penmanship was neat and purposeful and, aside from the overuse of the comma, there were only a few grammatical mistakes. There were no misspellings either, as if it was written with a dictionary on hand. From just the first paragraph, Ed Slattery knew the correspondence took time and it was carefully thought out and constructed.

Intrigued, Ed unfolded the rest of the letter as he sat back in his chair. It was, after all, the correspondence he had stopped waiting for, but secretly hoped would still show up in his mailbox.

After the failed attempt at reducing his sentence, Doug Bouch had now been behind bars in the Lake Erie Correctional Institution for almost a year. Ed was still curious how the crash Doug caused lived inside his head.

Sir, please know first and foremost how deeply sorry I am for your loss. I simply can't apologize enough for the loss of your wife and the injuries incurred by your sons. It's simply not possible for me to properly convey in words how much my heart breaks continually over the thoughts of you, the boys and your family. My having been involved in such a horrific accident haunts me constantly. I can't even begin to imagine how you, your sons and your family must feel about all of this. You simply can't understand how sincere my sorrow truly is. I can't apologize enough to make you feel any better, but I pray you, your sons and your family will accept one from the bottom of my heart.

I'd like to relay a few things to you before I close that I feel you should know. Sir, I don't know how religious of a man you are, but I am a deeply religious born again Christian. I am very active in my church and well thought of in my community. Having said that, please know that I pray for you, your sons and your family at least twice every day without fail. Often, it's more than that. Yet to this day, and I'm sure for the rest of my life, your wife, your boys, you, and your family are on my mind and in my prayers constantly.

Secondly, I'd like to let you know, for what it's worth, that after 30 years of driving truck, I had enrolled in and been attending college. I was directed to make myself available for your civil suit, which I did for nine months until I was told it was resolved. I could not bear the thought of anything like this ever happening again. In May of 2011 I started attending college full time for an electrical technologies associates degree. At 50, I was determined to start all over again to avoid driving truck. Sir, I have been married to my wife for 32 years. I simply could not imagine having to live without her. It's been hard enough to have been in prison separated from her after all these years, I could not fathom how you must feel being without your wife. When I think of your loss, I can't begin to imagine how you must feel. I'm so extremely sorry you have gone through that.

When I was incarcerated, my wife and I lost our only source of income. She had to quit watching our grandsons to go to work to bring money into the house. My children had to start paying for daycare for the grandchildren they simply can't afford. My point, if you'll forgive me, is that this has dramatically adversely affected my whole family. I feel that at least fractionally I can understand the suffering your family has incurred. Again, I'm so very sorry.

Sir, I'm in no way trying to compare my situation to yours. Your's [sic] truly is beyond my comprehension. Please just know that I sincerely ache every single day for your loss and for what those boys have gone through. I pray you, your sons, and your family get all the healing and blessing you all so richly deserve.

Bouch closed with "Sincerely," and signed the letter formally by printing and signing Douglas S. Bouch. Ed folded the letter back up and sat for a minute to take in what he had just read.

People can use religion to justify all types of atrocities in this world, whether it is physical harm, stubborn, or irresponsible ignorance, or even to pander to a dangerous political sect. Ed Slattery was not a religious man, at least not in a conventional way. While he understood the emotional draw, and respected its place, no one was going to pray for him or, as he saw it, pray away the responsibility of the violent creation of his new reality.

Doug Bouch said he was sorry a dozen times in his letter and Ed recognized it. In fact there was a large part of him that thought maybe sorry was enough. This man never meant to take Susan's life, Ed thought. He genuinely felt bad that Bouch was sitting in prison, but as he sat there and chewed on the two-page letter, he became annoyed. Ed reread Bouch's words three more times, each pass revealing more of the intent behind the carefully-crafted apology. Bouch said he didn't mean to compare his pain to Ed's, but Ed couldn't help but notice Bouch couldn't write enough about his own pain. Even more egregious, though, is that Bouch never at any point took responsibility for any of it.

Ed stewed in that thought for a few weeks before writing a reply. He read Bouch's words several more times and, again, each time revealed a more shallow response than he truly wanted from this man. Ed Slattery wasn't looking for revenge, he simply wasn't the kind of man that could harbor that kind of anger and resentment, but he wanted respect — in his life and in those he chose to surround himself with, he commanded it. Ed Slattery wanted Doug Bouch to respect his life and Susan's by taking responsibility. He wanted help shouldering the burden that was this new life of his.

Wednesday, January 9, 2013
Dear Doug,

First of all, you can call me Ed. Second of all, thank you for the letter. I know that was difficult.

I have no doubt you remember August 16, 2010, and will for the rest of your life. I don't know what to tell you about that, except don't let it eat you up. That does not honor Susan, the boys, or your family.

While I appreciate your letter, I think you spend too much time on your own predicament. I have plenty of sympathy for what your family is going through. It sucks, but you did that, not me. I don't think you are blaming me. But I am not sure that you are taking full responsibility for what happened that day. You said in court that the crash was 'unavoidable' and your letter says, 'having been involved in such an accident,' aren't quite taking full responsibility. Taking responsibility is saying the crash 'I caused, by my decisions and actions.'

I am not trying to heap on 'guilt' that isn't yours. It is yours, and I fear that neither of us can truly move on until you take full responsibility for the events of that day. I often tell my kids that I don't want the stories they try to tell around their apologies. Just say, I'm sorry, make amends, and move on. I also want them to know when they have made their amends, so they can move on. I wish that for you, Doug. Say I am sorry, make amends and move on.

Ed continued by asking what Bouch did the weekend before his shift back in August, 2010, and to understand how his lack of sleep routine caused the crash. There were real consequences to all of it, and he wanted Bouch to take responsibility. Ed suggested maybe Bouch speak to other truckers, telling his story as an example of what can happen. Ed wanted Bouch to further think about Estes's role in the crash, as well, and about an industry he says killed nearly four thousand people a year. Don't divert attention by talking about the actions of others, Ed pleaded to Bouch, accept what happened, why it happened, and the role he played in it.

Ed ended the letter simply, but powerfully, conveying he was not satisfied with what Bouch's mind's eye was seeing.

I would like to meet you in person, face to face. Let me know if that is something you'd like to do.

Mostly, Doug, I want us all to heal to the best of our ability. I want your family put back together again, and I want my family to be happy. Of course, we find happiness in each other and friends, but there is a hole that will never be filled. You can't fix that, so don't try.

I forgive you. Susan's family forgives you. Now, begin to forgive yourself.

Months would go by before the two men would correspond again. Ed didn't know the reason for the silence and, quite frankly, didn't have much time to think about it. He was building a house, sending one son off to college, and continuing to learn to care for his youngest. Matthew was struggling with his new school and wondered aloud why he wasn't with his friends at St. Joseph's, or planning on attending high school at Calvert Hall like Peter did. Matthew seemed to know he was different, but didn't quite want to accept it, yet. It was a mental battle affecting his self-esteem and his studies while still trapped in a house that reminded him daily of his limitations.

Ed needed to, wanted to, deal with that, and didn't give Bouch's plea to get out of prison early much more thought, certainly not after the two-page letter he thought was skirting his responsibility.

Still, prison never seems temporary. While in the country's first privatized prison, Bouch would later say he witnessed rape, beatings, and violent assaults on other prisoners. He said he'd been abused. He reported spending his first Thanksgiving in the infirmary after a man serving two life sentences put a master lock in a sock and hit him upside the head before beating him senseless.

Bouch said his belongings were stolen, his lock picked, and he was chastised for his religious beliefs. He said he would read his bible often, visit the prison chapel, and spiritually reach out to people. Bouch said it was his faith that helped guide him through his sentence, but he paid a price. Prisoners said men his age who clung to the bible were usually child molesters and with Bouch being in Level 2, or medium security, that was probably what he was. Bouch said the inmates had a nickname for the Lake Erie Correctional Institution: Gladiator School.

It wasn't a pleasant existence but Bouch's hardship would only be one supporting reason for his attorney to ask for judicial release in his case for the second time. A hearing on that latest motion was set to go before Judge Enlow on September 30, 2013. It was a hearing attorney Errol Can asked to push to a later date citing Ed's desire to continue speaking with Bouch. It was a suggestion made in Ed's last letter to Bouch in January.

It was mid-September, 2013 when another letter arrived from the Lake Erie Correctional Institution. Ed pulled it out of the mailbox, walked in the house and, again, laid it on his desk. He wasn't sure he wanted to read what Bouch had written. It took days before he did.

September 16, 2013
Dear Mr. Slattery,

I hope this letter finds you doing well. Before I begin I would like to apologize to you for my first letter. It seemed from your response I only further caused you hurt. That was never my intention, nor was there any intended play on words or avoidance of blame on my part. I was merely trying to walk on eggshells as it were so as not to cause you any more pain then I already had. Please accept my sincere apology.

It was also never my intention to come across as spending too much time on my predicament. I was trying to relay to you that I had indeed analyzed my decisions, the consequences, and was trying to explain to you what I had done to avoid this from ever happening again.

You asked what I did that day and the weekend before the crash. My weekend started Friday at about 2:00 p.m. when I got off work for the week. We had just moved so I worked inside the house putting things away, hanging pictures, etc. until late in the evening. Saturday we had the kids and grandkids out for a cookout. Sunday I slept in until about 9:30 a.m. and stayed home from church. I worked down at the barn most of the day mending and cleaning stalls. I went up to the house about 6:00 p.m. to get cleaned up, eat, and go to bed. I went to bed but couldn't sleep so I got back up until about 10:00 p.m. before I went back to bed. I returned to work Monday at 3:00 a.m.

As for my decisions…of course I wish I had decided differently, that day and the days leading up to it. I should have done several things differently. I shouldn't have worked so much at home after a long week at work. I should have went to bed earlier Sunday night. I should have stayed at the rest area longer that day. I should have taken a longer break in my run. I should have known better than to work the type of schedule I did. I wished I were not pulling triple trailers. Please don't take any of these as excuses. I'm far too aware of my poor choices to excuse them.

The last issue I would like to address is the responsibility aspect. You said "I fear that neither of us can truly move on until you take full responsibility for the events of that day." It was my thoughts that I had done that by signing a guilty plea, pleading guilty, and not trying to take this to trial. I did not know you wanted to hear me say the crash I caused by my decisions and actions as well, I sincerely thought I had done that. Again, I apologize to you.

Sincerely,
Douglas S. Bouch

And there it was.

Ed Slattery was not an idiot, and he was keenly aware of the seemingly impeccable timing between Errol Can's latest motion and Bouch's second letter, albeit nine months later, but Ed was also a man eager to forgive.

While certainly not a religious man, he was one of principle. In general, he believed it was easy to love people that love you. The challenge, he always believed, was to love those that hurt you.

Ed's challenge was to forgive the man who destroyed his life. Whether there was a God or not, Ed truly didn't know. The whole idea of Him or Her made no sense to him, but he did think that Buddha, Mahatma Gandhi, Jesus, and Mohammed couldn't all be wrong about absolution and compassion. No matter which book you read, Ed believed it was better to forgive than to harbor hate, anger, and vengeance.

All he wanted Bouch to do was clearly take responsibility for what he'd caused. Admit to himself and to Ed that his decisions caused a world of hurt for two families, and that maybe he would think about channeling that mistake into something more productive.

Ed was serious about that face-to-face, and still more serious about the two working together toward change in the trucking industry. In Bouch admitting fault and being "far too aware of his poor choices," Ed saw that glimmer of redemption he so badly was hoping to see. It is why he almost immediately sat down and penned the letter Bouch was so desperately seeking. While the timing of his letters and Bouch's attorney's motions were suspect at best, Ed was satisfied. He felt it was time to write Judge Enlow and express his family's opinion that Doug Bouch, indeed, deserved relief.

Judge John A. Enlow
Portage County Courthouse
203 West Main St.
Ravenna, Ohio 44266

Dear Judge Enlow,
It is my understanding that Doug Bouch is requesting an early release from prison.

I am writing in support of his request.

I was pretty clear in my original appearance at Doug's sentencing hearing in arguing that a prison sentence would send a clear signal to the industry, drivers in particular, about the dangers of driving tired. I think that has been accomplished.

Further, I see little benefit to Doug, my family, or the industry in his continued incarceration at this time. My wish is that Doug be allowed to return to his family and begin to pick up the pieces of his life.

Finally, and let me make it clear that this is not a quid pro quo for my support of his release, I would very much like to meet with Doug before his release and begin a dialogue about how he might be able to help us with our message about truck safety issues.

As I pointed out in his sentencing hearing, the trucking industry is involved in nearly 4,000 fatalities and tens of thousands of injuries every year. Nearly 700 of those deaths are the industry's own drivers. Anything Doug and I can do to lower these numbers is to the good, and Doug has a terrifying story to tell, i.e., your boss is going home to his family, you are going to jail. I'd like him to tell that story.

Please don't hesitate to call if you have any questions or concerns.

Sincerely,
Edward M. Slattery, Ph.D.

The letter was exhibit A in the last motion Errol Can would file on behalf of Douglas S. Bouch on January 16, 2014. Again asking for judicial release, Can argued as grounds for his latest motion the major financial hardship Bouch's family was suffering, because of his two years of incarceration, the several assaults Bouch claimed he suffered while in prison, and, most importantly, the "kindly written" letter from Mr. Edward Slattery to his Honor.

It may have been Ed Slattery's words that helped seal Doug Bouch's fate in January 2012, but it would also be Ed's words that would help free him almost exactly two years later.

Chapter 15

Doug Bouch did not like pickles.

On April 10, 2014, Bouch had his first meal outside prison walls in 27 months. He had been incarcerated for more than two years, and his first taste of freedom was a Whopper with cheese, medium Coke, and medium fries. No pickles.

The Burger King was just three miles outside the prison in Conneaut, Ohio and the first stop along a 172-mile, two-day journey that would end with Bouch standing before Judge John Enlow back in Portage County.

After several attempts at a judicial release, Bouch was being transported to attend a hearing on Friday, April 11th at 1 p.m. The last motion armed with Ed Slattery's personal letter to the judge worked, and Doug Bouch was to be a free man. His release was immediate. It was so ordered. Bouch was going home.

While not a shock, the news still jolted Ed. He didn't know what to think. He obviously advocated for Bouch's release and thought it was the right thing to do, but he was conflicted. Ed certainly knew this day would come, especially after the letter he wrote to the court. But now it was happening. In some small way the vindication he received over Susan's death was being lifted of his own volition. He wanted Bouch to go home, he truly did, but he also wanted to preserve the importance of his wife's death and her still very painful absence. It was an irrational thought, polar opposite, really, but it only served to illustrate the push and pull in Ed's conscience. It was one of the many intricacies of mourning and grief that worked to prevent healing, but also part of the emotional evolution of letting go. It was, Ed imagined, yet another cross to bear along his journey.

Still, Ed thought Bouch should have the opportunity to go home and pick up the pieces of his life much the way he himself was doing. After all, Ed was on his way home too, finally moving into the house he helped design and had built specifically for how his family was now constructed. Whatever healing there was to be done, it would happen here. Equal parts necessity for Matthew and homage to Susan, the house was the safe space Ed could afford to create.

The home was unique in not just function, but in appearance. It was an ultra-modern design warmed up with wood trim, reclaimed sliding barn doors, and dramatic arches offering loft space, and an open, airy concept. The communal area was beautiful, with a wall of windows looking out onto a private yard. Off the main space was an apartment for Ed's mother, should she need or want it. On the other side was a wing for Ed, Peter, and Matthew. Beyond the laundry room, the wing included the therapy pool and bedrooms for all three men along that massive concrete wall built into the hill. At the end of that hallway was the base of the meditation tower, a three story 12 x 12 structure that offered access to the plants and herbs on the green roof outside and, on the top floor, an outlook post with panoramic views of the Towson skyline. It came with a custom-installed assisted pulley system, so when Matthew was able, he could use his upper body to pull himself up to that special perch.

Outside was just as stunning, again modern, but softened by wood accents, including part of the roof. Ed didn't want the massive home to be obvious; he wanted the appearance of the size to fit in with the older homes in the established neighborhood. To look at it head on, that desire was accomplished. Also disguised was just how environmentally dynamic the house was. It was four-thousand square feet, with a fraction of the footprint, which was the envy of green homebuilders everywhere, and also a statement in Universal Design, which addresses the needs of the disabled, well above and beyond ADA compliancy.

Ed tirelessly researched products that could remove hurdles to Matthew's continued recovery and just about all of them, no matter the cost, were built into the home.

The design of smooth concrete floors, no swing open doors, sunken rugs, and wheelchair-proof baseboards proved a dream for navigating in Matthew's wheelchair. The kitchen was equipped with pull down cook tops and cabinets. Matthew's own bathroom was more of a seamless wet room with custom finished concrete benches and fixtures.

The house was built so Matthew would never have to want for anything the rest of his life, a life that started as soon as the family moved in. Instantly, Ed noticed Matthew's recovery accelerate. He could help cook, clean, shower, and made good use of the custom therapy pool. There were no more walls, doors, or lips in the floor impeding Matthew's movement. There was literally nowhere in or out of the home that Matthew couldn't get to. The problem for Ed was no longer where Matthew couldn't go, but where he did go. His son was liberated in form, function, and self-esteem. It was everything Ed thought he was building; the Slatterys were now living the life Ed architected from the very first sketch of the impressive home, even down to the memory of Susan.

The kitchen had concrete countertops custom-made by a talented artist, designer, and craftsman in Baltimore; poured and finished not only to accent the modern design of the home, but also to honor Susan Slattery. Along the side of the countertop was the number Pi. It was part of the mold during the process of making the tops and wrapped around the entire piece, allowing for 200 numbers of the infinite figure. It was subtle, but powerful, and, somehow, made the new house a true home.

As move-in day passed and time in the new home became a week, then a month and beyond, Ed and his family settled into a stride made possible only by the hurdles removed by design. It was noticeable, not just physically, but emotionally. Often, Ed found himself gently tracing the numbers of Pi molded into the countertop as he walked through the kitchen. Still wearing both his and Susan's rings on his left hand, he would listen as the gold bands together would scrape and trace against the curves and angles of 3, 1, 4, 1, 5, 9, 2... The home was built for Matthew's recovery, but tracing those numbers was Ed's therapy.

Still, Ed felt there was a lot of healing left to do. His family had finally made it home and, while a different journey entirely, Doug Bouch had just done the same. Two families then, nearly four years removed from the collision that so violently brought them together, were picking up and moving on, both as best they could.

~~~

Ed never got his face-to-face with Dough Bouch before his April 11th release, and he hoped maybe now that he was out of prison, the two men could meet, shake hands, and move on, either together or apart. Their correspondence through letters felt disjointed and lacked the kind of clarity needed to truly appreciate and understand the plight of either man. Ed understood that, in the bigger picture, Doug Bouch was a victim, too. Ed hoped to commiserate, but knew just how difficult a meeting could be for both men.

Ed had ideas of putting his entire ordeal into a book, and he knew the story would need Bouch's side of things. He asked me to broker the interview, not as a reporter for my television station, but rather, as a journalist and author he believed was the right storyteller.

I agreed with Ed, Doug Bouch was essential to telling this story. Well before we were deep into the process of research and interviews to write the beginning and middle, we knew we needed the end. I urged Ed to call Doug Bouch and schedule a time to meet now that he had been out of prison for a few months.

Ed had to summon the courage to cold call Doug Bouch. He did it several times. Setting up the meeting was not easy. There were a host of awkward messages left on machines and missed calls, but finally Ed and Doug spoke.

It was a brief conversation, terse...tense. There was not much to say when so much had already been said. But they agreed to meet when Ed would be in Ohio for the Palmer family reunion in August, 2014.

The terms were not warm, nor contentious; just two men who had some business left to tend to and lives that either needed to reconcile or be severed once and for all.

Chapter 16

"Can I take a look at your reservation, sir?" a voice said from the other side of my sunglasses, which had fogged up since emerging from the crisp air conditioning inside the rental car terminal at the Cleveland Airport.

I took my glasses off and handed the woman my receipt. She studied it for a second and in a terse, but respectful way, said, "Any car on the left between spots 10 and 20."

The options were typical, full size sedans by different makers that invariably looked like the same model. I walked toward the row and, again, looked down at my printed out reservation. My eye caught the date, August 16, 2014. In the rush to plan this trip and conduct this interview, I simply hadn't realized the importance of the date we chose. August 16, 2014; it was four years to the day. I stopped for a second, dumbfounded by the irony, and my lack of awareness of it, and looked at a clock on the wall. It was 10 a.m. I couldn't help but think four years ago, at that exact time, Ed Slattery was blissfully unaware he only had two hours left of a life he was about to lose.

"Sir! Which one are you going to take?"

The Alamo worker rattled me from my inner dialogue.

"Sorry," I said standing in front of a blue Mazda 6. "This one is just fine."

I hopped in the car and punched in the address of the Cleveland hotel where I was staying. I was to meet Ed Slattery in the parking lot, pick him up, and travel to meet the man who so violently altered the course of his life.

Doug Bouch had been out of prison for four months, and Ed Slattery wanted to see him. Ed wanted to talk to him, interview him, see his expressions, and experience his pain. Ed simply wanted to hear what life was like for the man and, maybe, if he was interested in working together to make trucking safer.

I arrived at the hotel and spotted Ed's van in the parking lot.

"Sir, are you ready?" I asked.

"It is now or never. Let's just go."

Ed jumped in the rental, and we drove the hour and forty-five minutes east from Cleveland to Greenville, Pennsylvania, to Doug Bouch's front porch.

Ed and I sat in near silence for most of the way out of the Cleveland metro area. If anything, we kicked around some small talk about the annual family reunion Ed was already in Ohio to attend, or something funny Matthew did or said. Ed always had a story about Matthew's continued awakening, both from his own brain and pubescence; either were always fodder for a good laugh. And laugh we did, until the scenery became rural. Suddenly, it no longer felt like a road trip. For Ed, it was increasingly clear it was a pilgrimage, or even a crusade.

After a quiet stretch of asphalt, I said what had been on his mind since I landed. "So, I know you know what today is," knowing full well, while it may have escaped me, it was locked away in Ed's brain.

Ed looked at the clock, which read 11:00 a.m.

"In about forty-five minutes, my wife was killed exactly four years ago," Ed said, looking back up at the road, "And I am headed to the doorstep of the man who did it."

Silence is not quiet in the aftermath of such powerful irony. The words echoed so loudly, it forced a reticent reflection for miles.

"I worry is all," Ed finally said, "You know, no one knows where I am and what we are doing. I didn't tell the kids, and I certainly didn't tell Susan's parents."

Ed looked out the window at the lush green scenery on the side of Highway 422 as we approached the Ohio-Pennsylvania state line.

"But I guess, selfishly, this is for me, anyway."

"How do you mean?"

"Well, it's been four years. Shit, in just a few minutes it will be four years to the damn second, and you know what? I'm not even sure I even had time to mourn my wife, yet. Still."

Ed sighed while continuing to look out the window. The weather on August 16, 2014 was much like August 16, 2010. It was sunny, clear, and beautiful. Ed had his left arm resting on his left knee and the near-noon August sun was just low enough in the late-summer sky to cause a reflection of the two wedding rings Ed still wore. It shimmered for just a second, causing Ed to look down.

"I guess in some way this crazy trip might provide some semblance of closure. Maybe, just maybe, if I see that Doug mourns and takes responsibility for the loss of Susan's life because of the choices he made, then I can put her to rest in my own mind. Maybe."

Truth is, Ed Slattery didn't know what to expect on the front porch of Douglas S. Bouch. The only sure thing was that he needed to do it. He was insistent. It was always the plan in his mind, but meeting Bouch on the exact anniversary of the crash he caused was only unintended and erratic drama; a Shakespearian type kismet playing out on a theatre in the round much like the Globe, surrounded by an audience of pain, grief, tragedy and, maybe, like a true Shakespeare play, a small chance at redemption for the villain.

Ed wanted so badly to forgive Doug Bouch to his face and for Bouch to ask Ed for it, if not by saying those exact words, then by showing even the slightest remorse for decisions he made that fateful morning. Ed needed to know the human condition still bonded him to people like Bouch. In all of what he learned in the four years since losing his wife, his sons as he knew them, and the life he worked so hard to get right, he just wanted to know Bouch learned much of the same. It was becoming clear in the moment to Ed that this was more for him than it was Doug Bouch.

Ed needed to believe there was a greater purpose in the tragedy beyond how it physically and emotionally affected his life and he traveled all the way to Greenville, Pennsylvania to find it. He wanted a partner in tragedy, one who would add color to the shadows of his own story to better complete a picture to show the world. Ed thought that together, the men just might be able to heal each other's lives with the pieces each had left from the crash. Together their story could be whole enough to illustrate a need for change.

"Well listen, I want to get this out of the way now before we get any closer," I said. "You asked me to come along to document this moment and broker the interview. I know this is going to be incredibly emotional, but I need you to let me lead and conduct. You want his side of the story, and you need to let me get it from him, no matter what it may be. I need you to be calm and collected while I ask the questions."

"I think considering the circumstances, I am remarkably calm," Ed responded.

He was. The day, while brilliant outside, felt dreary and grim, heavy with emotion and irony, but Ed had the mark of a man with intent. He was consistent, cool, and eager.

Finally we arrived in Greenville. It didn't take long to find the street and the house, shorter then Ed would have liked. I could feel him pull back.

"Am I ready for this?" Ed asked me, as I parked the car a half a block away.

"We can sit here all day and you will never be ready for this. The situation makes you ready."

It's true, but easier for me to say.

We got out of the car and approached the modest duplex. While walking up to the porch, everything Ed had envisioned he wanted this moment to be flashed out of his mind. No longer was this an intellectual exercise; it was an emotional one becoming more visceral with each step toward the door.

Ed knocked once and we both stood back. About twenty seconds went by and still no answer, no movement from behind the door.

Ed leaned in and knocked again. Still nothing. Time, money, emotion, too much was invested in what was supposed to be on the other side of that door. The letdown was too far of a drop for Ed to fathom, it most certainly couldn't be that way; it shouldn't be that way. He wanted, he needed...

The door flew open.

"Oh, hi, Ed, I thought you were gonna call," Bouch said with such an ease, it almost robbed the meeting of its drama.

"Oh, no," Ed said, "We said noon on the phone the other day, don't you remember?"

The two men studied one another for one of those seconds that felt more like a minute. It was the first time they had laid eyes on each other since Bouch was sentenced and, more importantly, the very first time they locked eyes. There was much said between these two men in letter form, but so much more was being communicated as they faced one another squarely for the very first time.

Ed stood there in a collared blue button-down shirt tucked into khakis and boat shoes. As presentable as Ed looked, Bouch clearly wasn't expecting anyone, or simply didn't care. He was wearing loose shorts and a ragged old tee-shirt. He was barefoot, his beard needed grooming, and his hair was longer and redder then Ed remembered.

"No, I thought you would call," Bouch said, "Well, let me check with my wife real quick to see if we can do this."

He explained how the couple was off to friends or family for the afternoon, and disappeared behind the door and up the stairs.

"The other day we agreed at noon on Saturday. I am not sure what this is all about," Ed said to me.

The door opened again and Bouch stepped out onto the porch.

"Well, I would invite you both inside, but my wife wants nothing to do with this, which I am hoping you understand. I mean, if this won't take long we can do it right here on the porch, if you all want to pull up a chair."

Ed was quiet, put off by how cavalier Bouch was acting toward a moment he had built up in his head.

"This is fine," I interjected quickly sensing both Ed's annoyance and that Bouch's desire to speak on the record was dubious at best, "this will work just fine."

Doug sat in a chair right by the front door while Ed took a seat near the railing of the porch. I popped open my laptop and a sheet with some prepared questions I knew Ed wanted answered. I hadn't been in a position exactly like this before but I know when an interview subject has limited patience for production or process, and I worked quickly so as to not give him the option of walking away. After all, I was in the middle of two men whose current lives were the direct result of the other, for better and worse.

It was no man's land for an interviewer. The tension was thick, and the air volatile, like in the moments just before a summer thunderstorm. The two men were cordial but nervous. The enormity of what was happening was starting to set in and manifest itself in a pithy, yet ancillary, conversation between the two men, while I hurriedly set up my laptop, and an external microphone on a side-table I'd asked Bouch if I could use.

The nervous chatter was running out. There was clearly not much left to say about the weather or the drive. Then Ed began to talk about some of the research he had done over the years about trucking and fatigue.

"First night back is difficult," Ed said referring to the shift Bouch was driving for Estes, "and this is something…"

"It's the easiest one of the week," Bouch interrupted to disagree.

"Well the data shows there are more crashes on first night back than any other night of the week, so we know that, in fact, that is a difficult transition to make," Ed responded.

The interview was jumping on me. I didn't want them to go down this road, not yet. Order. A script would be the only thing to keep it from deteriorating into an emotional abyss, I thought to myself as I put my hands up like a referee to stop play.

"Gentlemen, let me take control here of what is going on for a second."

I reminded Mr. Bouch that he agreed to this interview and it was for a book on the matter. "We are just gonna have a conversation," I said, "I am just going to ask a couple questions, we're just gonna talk, okay?"

It was a standard line I used for when I interviewed anyone who wasn't used to microphones and cameras to ease any nerves. Bouch matter-of-factly pushed through it.

"Well, I thought that was what we were just doing," he chuckled.

Still, I started easy to diffuse the tension by asking Bouch about how he grew up and how he got into trucking. Start small, diffuse nerves. Tell me about yourself.

"I've been driving for thirty years now. I mostly got into it because that's what my brothers did. When I got out of school, rather than go to college, I wanted to go to work. My brothers already worked at a trucking company, and I went to work on the dock at the trucking company."

Bouch said ultimately Estes hired him in 1998, and that it was regarded in the industry as a good company.

"Excellent company," Bouch said. "Best place I had worked in thirty years."

Bouch said he got paid $0.53 a mile for his line haul duties, which he maintained was higher than the average industry rate. He was pulling down just more than $1500 a week. Estes was the top of the industry, he said, good work if you can get it, and a company which he made a point to continue to defend, despite the fact he no longer worked for them.

"That's part of the stigma that goes along with this," Bouch said. "Ed had made a comment before that, well, ya know, isn't kind of sad that here I am in my situation, and you are in your situation, and Estes is going happy down the road. Other than to force me to drive the triples—which I didn't care to drive the triples —but, other than forcing me to drive the triples, [on that day or] any other day, they didn't force me to drive illegal, or do anything that was outside regulations. There is no big bad Estes involved."

Blame was not the narrative Bouch was willing to entertain. Not for the company he no longer worked for, not even himself. Despite the evidence that put him in jail for two years and, perhaps even more brazen, despite the goodwill of the man who helped get him out early, Bouch was beginning to chart an entirely different course in the interview.

He was losing patience with my preliminary, but necessary, questions about his route on August 16, 2010, his load that day, and how far he traveled. At times, I repeated myself to make sure I got his version right.

"So, total mileage for that day was going to be what again?"

"532," he said, annoyed.

Ed piped up as if to commiserate with Doug, "You got to be patient with him. He's a journalist," Ed said jokingly, trying to ease Bouch's growing irritation.

"I hate repeating myself," Doug said, "No, no, I hate repeating myself. It is a pet peeve of mine. Somebody asks you a question and then they don't listen to the answer. Why ask me the question if you're not going to listen to the answer?"

It was clear he was becoming a little agitated.

"I'm just trying to get the facts right." I responded.

I am not sure he meant anything personal by it, but it was clear Doug Bouch wanted to move on.

"So, take me to the accident," I asked switching gears, "What do you remember from it, step by step. You're traveling eastbound on I-80?"

"Yup, and I got to the 191 mile marker," Bouch began, "Before you topped the hill, there was a sign on the right hand side and it said there was construction two miles ahead," Bouch said..

Preparing to lose two lanes, Bouch explained how he moved into the center lane and tapped off the cruise control to slow down. As he topped a hill, he said he saw all the traffic backed up and stopped. That is when he stood on his brakes.

"I just simply couldn't get stopped."

Bouch explained he was underweight that day at 103,000 pounds and, as he remembered, he put down 264' of skid marks.

Ed knew the accident report well enough to know the numbers weren't adding up. The Ohio State Highway Patrol measured 93' of skid marks, signifying a far less prepared stop than what Bouch was recalling. There was also no hill mentioned in the accident report, either, and definitely no crest that could hide the view of a bottleneck. Still, it was his side Ed wanted to hear, and he sat stoically and expressionless, and listened as Bouch continued.

"I realized I wasn't gonna get the truck stopped in time. I couldn't put it on either side. There wasn't anywhere for me to go, the whole thing all the whole way across was blocked up."

"Do you remember the impact?" I asked.

"Yeah," Bouch responded, "I can tell you where I put the truck. I purposefully put the truck where it impacted."

There was nothing he could have done to prevent it, he continued. Each lane, and even the shoulder, was blocked with cars, and he had to hit somewhere. Bouch explained he thought he slowed down more than enough, and it all came up so quickly, there was nothing he could have done. It was in the skid, when he chose to impact where he did.

"There's a slot. You're looking across this whole thing," he explained illustrating with his hands, "There is nowhere to go. Between the pickup truck and Susan's car, which was right behind the Covenant truck in the center lane, there was a gap."

It was the first time Bouch mentioned Susan by name. While his tone didn't much change, his facial expression nearly winced at the proper mention of her. It was a fleeting moment, but also a telling one, as he recovered to finish the explanation.

"There's a gap," he said, "I knew the truck wasn't going through it without impact, but there was a clean shot."

Bouch explained if he could get through that gap, he would be able to get to the jersey wall and hit the minimal amount of people. To go anywhere else would have caused even more damage, he said.

Bouch said he figured Susan's car would bounce off the back of the Covenant truck's rear drop guard, or ICC bumper, and off to the side. Instead, from high up in his cab, he saw his truck push her right up and under the corner as he blew through the opening.

Bouch remembered seeing the red Ford Focus crumble up underneath the other semi. From his vantage point, he saw his split-second decision physically and violently end a human life on his way through that "slot."

Bouch then continued to recall how his truck slammed into the jersey wall and caught fire. He explained how he expended one full fire extinguisher from his cab, but it wasn't enough. Walking to the back of his truck he could see the carnage the triple left in its wake, including EMS workers near Susan's car. He said he stayed by the jersey wall, because he didn't want to get in the way, nor did he want to know what was going on in Susan's vehicle.

But Bouch must have known exactly what was going on in that mangled Ford Focus. He knew, because he watched the last seconds of Susan Slattery's life from the perch of his rig.

"To be involved in something that horrific," Bouch said turning to Ed with tears in his eyes, "There aren't any words, and there is nothing I can say to you." The weight of the moment stood still, encased in Bouch's pause, as he choked back more tears.

Ed stood stoic, yet compassionate, telling him to take his time. Bouch did, but it wasn't necessarily to emotionally recover or offer condolences to the man sitting on his porch. He wanted Ed to know there was another victim in that crash.

"You don't understand," Bouch said as he continued to choke back tears, "You take somebody who's been what I've been my whole life, the kind of person I've been, done things the way I've done them, and to be the horrible, big, bad, unlawful, ignorant truck driver, that couldn't have been any further from the truth. If you had known me prior to the accident, you woulda said wow, what a guy. Look at the way he conducts himself. Look at the way he lives his life. Look at the way he goes above and beyond for everything and everybody," Bouch said with a voice increasingly solid with confidence, as he broke out of the prior emotional tailspin.

"I might still say that, Doug," Ed said, "At no point did I ever think you were a big, bad truck driver. At no point did I think you were awful, lazy, mean-spirited. At no point did I ever think you got up that morning thinking this was going to happen. So please, understand that feeling you are getting, you are not getting from me."

Ed looked at Bouch and saw a hard-working, blue-collar man who built a career doing honest work to raise a family. Not entirely unlike himself. Ed wanted to make it clear he was sympathetic to Doug's plight in all of this as well.

"Do I think your industry is a little out of control? Yes, I do. Do I think you're out of control? Not necessarily. I think that you are in a system that sucks."

But Bouch bowed up in his chair to disagree with Ed's thesis, "Regardless of what kind of industry I was in, I was in total compliance in every aspect of what I was doing."

Bouch said it with such confidence it almost made his words that much more irresponsible.

"Wait a second, Doug," I interrupted. I saw Ed losing his composure. I maintained the role of referee, both for the rising emotions, and the altered version of the truth Bouch was beginning to adopt.

"But the trooper that took the statement from you, I have the report right here..."

"Yeah you know, I got out of prison on April 17th of this year. It was sometime in January, I don't remember exactly when, my pastor came up. That was the first time I had ever read that statement," Bouch said.

"So you don't remember giving that statement to the trooper on the scene? That you fell asleep?" I asked.

"Oh I gave a statement. I remember very well what I said. I never told him I fell asleep."

Suddenly, realities were being rewritten. What was given fact for four years was simply not how Doug Bouch saw it anymore.

"So what that implies is that the trooper..." Ed couldn't even finish his dumbfounded response to Bouch's previous statement before he finished his thought.

"Misrepresented me. Absolutely," Bouch said, before continuing, "I think what he did was he took some liberties and filled in some things, because I made the statement to him that, ya know..." Bouch paused. He was fidgeting in his chair. He looked back up at me and said, "I went like that."

Bouch demonstrated and closed his eyes for a beat or two longer than normal before he reopened them. As he focused back on me, he said, "I had a long blink of an eye."

Bouch was describing what experts call a "microsleep." It can last from a fraction of a second to ten seconds. It is an unintended brief sleep, usually broken by a head bob or snap, but traveling at 60 miles per hour, those couple of seconds can mean hundreds of yards.

"Were you tired?" Ed asked.

"No," he responded. "I just told him [trooper] when I topped the hill, I had a long blink of an eye. It wasn't anything out of the norm. It happens constantly."

Bouch basically accused the trooper of taking a false report that helped throw him in jail. It seemed so far-fetched, but it was a storyline he was rewriting in his own head. The skid marks were longer in his version, there was a hill that prevented him from seeing what was coming up, he didn't fall asleep, he simply blinked, and that trooper... well, the trooper must have had some political motivation, because people don't like triples in Ohio. Doug Bouch wasn't just rewriting what was all public record, he was reimagining it.

He said he pleaded guilty only because he was promised five years' probation and no prison time. He explained he had already started school to get his associates degree in electrical technologies, and wanted to leave his previous career, and the pain it caused him, in the rear view mirror.

Suddenly, it was *he* who had suffered. Prison wasn't kind to a man his age. Bouch detailed how he was beaten and questioned because of his daily visits to the chapel and reading of the Bible. But what haunted him most was the nightmare. A nightmare, he explained, he still suffered three to four times a week.

"I wake up right before impact," Bouch said, with tears in his eyes.

"I remember topping the hill. I see the sign at the top of the hill, and I wake up right before impact."

Bouch was as pained as he was angry about his recurring dream and the entirety of the situation that caused it, as he seemed to be recreating it.

Ed remained quiet through all of it. He wanted to hear where Bouch's head was at and learned it was not in any agreed-upon reality.

"I didn't have to go through this," Bouch said, "There was not anything that I could have done differently. There wasn't anything I should have been doing differently to have avoided the accident."

It was the recurring excuse Ed heard from Bouch at his sentencing, in their correspondence, and now, again, in person. It was the one thing Ed simply could not accept about August 16, 2010. There was no intent in Doug Bouch, Ed knew that, but there was definitely negligence, and he was the reason Ed no longer had his family.

Doug continued, "One side was done on purpose and the other side was a pure, unavoidable..."

Doug was going to say the word accident, but Ed interrupted. He could sense Bouch skirting responsibility again and now seemed to be indicating that Ed purposefully sought vengeance, which brought Bouch's family and himself so much pain.

It was clear Ed had had enough and was about to take over the interview. I was inclined to let him. He had already shown so much restraint, but I stopped him. I had one more question I felt I needed to ask.

"Do you feel remorseful?"

It needed to be asked. I saw remorse in this man's eyes. He cried, he hurt, and he seemed irrevocably damaged by the events of that day, but Doug's answer was not what I expected...not what Ed wanted to hear.

"The biggest problem that I had in all of this...and I don't know how else to say this...It took me a long time to get over the fact that God used me as the vehicle to take her life."

The statement left Ed speechless at first before he recovered from the sucker punch. As maddening as Bouch's assertions and selective recall were to that point, the divinity excuse was the most insane.

"Well, that is where theologically we would differ. God did not set that day for Susan to die. That is not a God I believe in. God does not choose the day that you are going to die," Ed said.

"I think the Bible says differently, but we will just let that be."

"Right, okay," Ed said as his brain retreated to logic in the face of such offensively blind faith, "but what bothers me about that statement, is that you're very focused on why God chose *you* to kill Susan, but it doesn't bother you to ask why God chose that to be Susan's day."

Ed was trying to understand how Bouch was able to convince himself that he was the only victim, and Susan, his love, was merely a character in God's play of Doug Bouch's life.

"Isaiah 55 says my ways are not your ways. Your thoughts are not my thoughts," Bouch quoted, as if to just rationalize away what sounded insane to Ed. "It's not for me to question," Bouch continued, "That's one of the reasons why I had such a big problem, theologically, with it, because I was questioning Him. I was asking. I wanted to know."

"So, are you at peace with the fact that this was just God's plan for your life?" Ed asked.

"No, I hate it. I hate it."

"No, you hate me, not God," Ed said "I did not choose this for you."

"I disagree," Bouch said sternly, steadfast in his belief that crushing Susan's life underneath his rig was simply God's plan; it is what the Almighty wanted.

Bouch's words froze the quickening moment. It was clear the fifty-two-year-old convinced himself he was the innocent victim. Not only did he feel God chose him as the vessel to take Susan, because it was her time, but he also blamed Ed's grief and his statement in court for putting him in prison.

Doug Bouch 'accidentally' did not get enough sleep the night before the crash. He 'accidentally' took a "long blink of an eye." It was an 'accident' that he aimed for Susan's car, and it was certainly an honest mistake that he snuffed out her life as he crushed her up under the stopped Covenant Lines truck. But Ed Slattery purposefully grieved publicly enough to put Doug Bouch in prison. It seemed in Bouch's version of Christianity, the tragedy was Ed Slattery's fault. It was a belief Ed simply could no longer tolerate to hear.

"Well now, you see, going on the facts that I had, I still stand by the statement that I made," Ed said.

"But you're the only one that did anything purposefully," Bouch responded.

"That just absolutely blows my mind," Ed said.

Bouch sat up in his chair, "I didn't get up that morning and say, you know what, to heck with the world, I'm going to go out there and be careless, and whatever happens, happens." Bouch's voice started to strengthen, "I didn't choose anything. You purposefully got up and chose to demand prison time."

The tone changed. Civility faded as both men quickened their speech and began raising their voices. It was clear this was no longer an interview so much as it was becoming a confrontation.

"I didn't demand anything, first of all," Ed said, "Second of all, you don't know that the judge would or would not have done, regardless of what I said. Your lawyer can say that I did, that I'm what tipped the balance. Your people can tell you that it was a vendetta against the American Trucking Associations. Your people can tell you whatever they want. That has got *nothing* to do with the truth. Did my statement sway the judge? I don't know," Ed said, as he shrugged his shoulders.

"Your letter is what got me out, so why didn't your statement sway it to begin with?" Bouch asked, as if it was a trick question of which only he held the answer.

"Maybe it did," Ed said.

"So the only person that purposefully did anything in all of this was you. You screwed me, you screwed my family," Bouch said in a matter-of-fact tone that made clear to Ed there would be no further reasoning with a man who he thought was clearly using religion to skirt responsibility. If reality were suspended in pure belief, logic would be no weapon, but it was still all Ed had.

"Let me ask you something, Doug. You said there was nothing that you could have or should have done differently that day. Why did the Covenant truck not hit anybody?"

"He was already stopped," Doug said.

"Right!" Ed blurted out, "He saw the construction signs, he slowed down, he managed to keep his truck under control, but you didn't. I taught my kids to drive, and what I taught them was, if you hit somebody else from behind, it's your fault. You were not in control of your vehicle."

"Well," Doug said, leaning back in his chair, "you don't understand what you're talking about when it comes to a truck."

At that moment, Ed was through with reason. Logic wasn't working, so maybe emotion would.

"My problem is you killed my wife," he said, "You. Killed. My. Wife. You did not have your truck under control."

"That's garbage!" Bouch shot back.

"You can rationalize that any way you want. There isn't a person on this planet, a reasonable person on this planet, who could justify the fact that you hit somebody else from behind," Ed said as he grew increasingly flustered.

Bouch met him at his level, "You made the statement that you don't call it an accident. What do you call it?"

"I call it a crash, because it wasn't an accident. It wasn't an 'on purpose.' I don't believe you did it on purpose, but somewhere between an accident and on purpose is this thing called a crash and that was avoidable!"

"I put two and a half million miles on my butt. Clean. Safe. No problem," Bouch shot back.

It was yet another discrepancy in his story, another half-truth he used to convince himself of his innocence, or God's will, or whatever else got him out of dealing with the very human consequences of the choices he made on this Earth. Bouch had a troubled driving record with Estes, and Ed knew it. But it didn't matter, not at that point, not on Doug Bouch's porch. What mattered was what Ed traveled to Greenville, Pennsylvania to say.

"You killed my wife. You! Nobody else."

"You want to know something, Ed?"

"You!" Ed exclaimed cutting Bouch off, "You killed my wife!"

"This is over. Get outta here. Get outta here!"

"You can't handle it!" Ed shouted.

"I'll tell you what I can't handle! I can't handle you screwing over me and my family, I didn't do anything purposefully to you, against you or Susan!"

"My son is in a wheelchair for the rest of his life. He can't even TALK TO ME!"

"Go away!" Bouch said sternly before repeating himself more threateningly, "GO AWAY!"

Ed walked past Doug on his way his way out, but not without saying his last words. "I hope someday you can say —"

"I HOPE YOU BURN IN HELL!" Bouch erupted, cutting off Ed's final words.

Ed absorbed the anger and simply finished his thought, "I hope someday you can say, 'I killed Susan,' and you can live with that."

"No, that is NEVER gonna happen!" Bouch shouted back.

We hurried toward the car. What had begun as an attempt at a civil conversation became anything but.

But Bouch wasn't done. Ed looked back over his shoulder at the porch and Doug was angrily pacing. Bouch caught eyes with Ed one more time and shouted down the street, "Don't you ever bother me again! That's right! Walk away!"

Ed turned his head and continued walking away. He was angry, but knew turning around or re-engaging Bouch wouldn't end well.

Then, Doug belted one last salvo as we got to the car, "SCREW YOU, BOY!"

Ed paused for a second before opening the car door. It was a shrill, schoolyard bully taunt, and it only further revealed to Ed just who he was dealing with.

We got in the car and drove off. Headed back west toward Cleveland, Ed's adrenaline was pumping. He was clammy, anxious, and trying to process the last few minutes of a confrontation he wouldn't soon forget.

It was quiet for a while. Ed's breathing began to slow back to normal, but I knew it masked the anxiety still running circles through his head.

"Get me back to the scene," he said, "I want to run the route that he ran that day. I want to see it again for myself. Get me to mile marker 190."

I took a left off route 422 to get back down to the Ohio Turnpike. We weren't far off. It didn't take long to reach the eastbound ramp near Streetsboro.

"Go. Drive," Ed said, as we merged onto I-80. "Okay, see that? This is mile 187. Three more."

The day began to take on a late afternoon glow. The sun was lower in the sky and shimmering off the flat pavement. Only the mirage effect of the heat rising off the blacktop offered any distortion of a straight path. Interstate 80 looked deserted. The road was clear, wide open, and smooth.

"Fucking hill," Ed muttered as he took out his phone and began to record, "I will show you. See, no hill."

Ed was trying to find some small speck of reason in the absurdity Doug Bouch had spewed forth, using the only trusty weapon he'd ever used in life, logic. It was futile, and perhaps he knew it, but it wasn't going to stop him from trying to see what

Bouch said he saw that day exactly four years ago. Only, Ed wouldn't, couldn't.

As we approached mile marker 190, Ed put his phone back in his pocket. He became quiet, reflective, as he watched the small green rectangle with the numbers 1, 9, 0 pass by the side window.

"Right...here," he whispered.

Ed wasn't going to see what Doug Bouch saw that day. As a man who subscribed to coherent reality, he never would.

The only thing Ed Slattery did see at that mile marker on August 16, 2014 were the remnants of two families now headed in opposite directions as violently as the collision that brought them together exactly four years ago. It was a potent physical and emotional reaction, caused by mixing religion, self-preservation, and denial with an attempt at closure, forgiveness, and confidence in the human condition. Jagged parts of those now lay in the road at mile marker 190.

Two families eviscerated; forever connected and yet severed in just one long blink of the eye.

Dear Susan,

I just returned from visiting Doug Bouch, the man who killed you. He spent over two years in prison and didn't fair too well from what I had heard and he now confirms. I was hoping that we could help each other heal and maybe even work together to talk to other drivers about fatigue and its consequences.

I was shocked to find out that he doesn't think he did anything wrong that day and that God had assigned this as your day to die. I was incredulous but sat through his bullshit. He actually had the gall to blame his imprisonment on me – 'you're the only one who had a choice to make in this whole affair. Susan and I had no choices, but you chose to tell the judge to put me in jail.'

Get this one — I reminded him that I wrote the letter that got him out more than two years early, and he said 'why'd it take you twenty-seven months?' I can feel my heart racing and hands tingling as I write this to you now.

I don't even remember what I said, but I did finally confront his story, and he blew up at me, and we hollered at each other a bit. I remember saying 'you killed my wife' several times as he retreated into his house and I began to follow him. I was never really tempted to touch him, but I knew it was getting out of control, so we turned to leave, at which point, he was yelling for me to burn in hell and get off his property.

Driving back to your parent's house, I was insistent that Brian and I re-trace the four miles before and through the site. It felt horrible, but I had to read the accident report again, because the things he was saying didn't make any sense and, as per the accident report, they were just flat out wrong.

I so wanted to forgive him and make something good out of this personal tragedy of ours, but it is not to be, so I just have to make peace with you. I'm not sure how to do that. I wasn't a perfect husband, I know, but we were always faithful to each other. Neither of us would have ever given up on the other. We loved our boys to the moon and back, I daresay maybe you a little more, if such comparisons can ever be made.

I don't know that I believe you are watching over us, hopefully you avert your eyes on occasion, but if you are, I hope you approve of the way I have carried on with our lives. In some ways, Matthew's the easy one. I know what he's doing at all times. He's still recovering, and the bond between us is tighter than ever. Of course, Peter is on a completely different path, and he is separating from home in significant and healthy ways. I just don't like it and don't respond to it very well sometimes. I just hope he understands that it's out of love, and some hurt, for what has happened to him, too.

In any case, my love, we are moving on, but we'll always miss you and never resolve the misfortune that befell us on August 16, 2010. There is no closure, just moving on.

I simply cannot imagine a day for the rest of my life that doesn't include thoughts of you.

Love,
Ed

Chapter 17 - The Last Word

Ed called the meeting with Doug Bouch a "holy shit moment." He likened it to committing unintended mischief as a child, like when you wanted to throw a rock at a neighbor's door, but missed and hit a window. That day in the car, driving away from Greenville, Pennsylvania, it felt like a rush, a panic. It may be because Bouch didn't make sense. Ed was shocked at what he'd heard and, after listening to the man explain away his role in Susan's death, Ed was seething. His heart rate was up, adrenaline pumping. He was left with fight or flight in the face of what he could only categorize as pure and gross ignorance.

It would take years for Ed's heart to stop racing from that meeting with Doug Bouch. After all, he had placed such import on it. Ed wanted it to resolve so much of the pain and confusion he had been feeling for so long. He simply didn't count on not having a willing, or damn near, obstinate participant.

Optimism and faith in Man, after all, is the one last innate insight we have left by our middle age. Belief that good will prevail over evil is the firewall that keeps us from losing hope. The idea that most people are decent and, given the chance, we are a forgiving and loving species that can't be easily eroded by the passing decades of our increased cynicism. Optimism doesn't go gray; faith doesn't wrinkle.

It was perhaps the one tenet of the humanity that remained intact for Ed, as he began his new journey in August of 2010. It was, quite literally, all he had left from his prior life. Everything around him changed in such a traumatic way. Lesser men would have folded, given up, or regressed into a depression. Ed was stronger than all of it, but leaned heavily on that innate belief that good is great, that good is what can come of such sadness, that good, indeed, was the politics of our human nature. Through all of it, the hospitals, the surgeries, the new home, and the world he was forced to recreate around his disabled son... it was that simple faith that kept Ed right-side up.

It was the principle that guided him, and he was hoping to find its validation in the confrontation with the man who was charged with taking it all from him. Ed wanted to know, he needed to know, that Doug Bouch was a good and honest person. He needed to know if Doug was remorseful, that he knew he was responsible, that maybe, Bouch, too, would ride the pain of what happened to a greater and more meaningful outcome— that Susan hadn't died in vain, and maybe Matthew's life-long struggle wouldn't be so tragically random.

It is, however, important not to confuse this notion with closure. Closure is an over simplified theory, a solution used as an antiseptic to kill the spores of complex emotion. It wasn't closure Ed was really after, it was meaning; reason. It was as much as the "why?" as it was the "I'm sorry." Ed wanted someone to take responsibility for his crushing loss, and he hadn't yet gotten it. Estes Express Lines settled a historic settlement, but that also meant the company wouldn't have to admit anything. The admitting a mistake would have to come from Bouch. It didn't.

"I was hoping that he was going to apologize," Ed told me. "I was going to tell him that I was so sorry that this happened to him because I *am* sorry that this happened to him, that he made choices, and it went very badly. So yeah, that's what I was expecting to happen. We were gonna hug and potentially talk to other truckers about how you don't want to do this. 'Prison ain't for you. Your boss is going to go home to dinner, and you're going to jail.' That was my intent."

Ed wanted people to learn from his cautionary tale, amplified by the cooperation of the very man who the state of Ohio blamed for caused it. It may seem naïve in hindsight, but

Ed pictured the two of them changing laws and the industry together. It was, four years to the day after the crash it turned out, Ed's shot at peace, or being at peace with what happened.

Intention, often, is just poorly designed optimism. The combustible meeting between the two men only served to drive them apart almost as violently as their lives had collided. It took months before Ed could view that confrontation sanely or apply any reason to it.

"Susan's death was easy, in a way" he said, "It's final. It's Matthew I grieve for every day. He's my constant reminder."

Matthew is a reminder that, in the end, the Slatterys tragedy was pure happenstance. Doug Bouch made the decisions he made, Estes Express Lines ran the routes it did the way it did, and Matthew is the living result. $40.8 million cannot, and will not, ever really square that in a way that makes sense of his loss.

Ed calls it the razor's edge.

"You're walking on this really thin ledge," he said. "On the left is this wonderful world with this kid, this guy who makes me laugh, who loves me, and whom I adore, and whose accomplishments I revel in. But on the other side, is the same kid with all the things he should be doing, but he isn't doing. Matthew should be graduating high school, going to prom, getting drunk, getting laid, and getting his drivers license. He will never do those things, at least not in a normal way. That is my razor's edge, fall to the left and everything is rosy, fall to the right and everything is scary."

It is the line Ed knows he will precariously straddle the rest of his life, and Doug Bouch wasn't about to help him balance.

"I am never going to hear Doug Bouch say 'I am sorry for the choices I made.' He is sorry Susan is dead, but he is not sorry he did it. So the question is, what's next?"

It didn't take long for Ed to begin to cobble together an answer. He, first and foremost, continued to focus on Matthew by mentally logging each and every accomplishment. They are almost always small steps, but they deserve the same kind of fanfare of a prideful father in his child athlete. Matthew is never going to hit a home run or throw a touchdown. His athletic prowess is limited to incrementally regaining the use of his right hand. Still, it takes determination and sheer will to purposefully attempt even the most routine movements with Matthew's right side, yet it is often his decision to do so. Matthew would rather use his disabled right hand to push his glasses up from the tip of his nose with his pointer finger. A motion he can easily do with his left side, but he chooses to stare down his right hand and, for what seems like ten minutes, will his hand to slowly push those glasses back up where they belong.

It is a determination any parent would be proud of, a feat more physically impressive than a block, a three-point shot, or a breaking ball for a called strike three. Matthew has made great strides since the crash. In many ways he is the same kid he was before it. Matthew is happy. He laughs, makes jokes, and possesses a wit that, if you're too patronizing with your conversation, he will gladly expose.

Matthew is much improved, physically. Ed believes the house he built has a lot to do with his development. Matthew likes to walk around the house with his walker and has taken to swimming and biking with special equipment for exercise. However, he remains severely handicapped and needs intense assistance to accomplish all of it, but he remains determined to achieve it, no matter the level of effort it takes.

Peter, too. For all his injuries and setbacks from the crash, Peter recuperated fully to not only graduate high school on time, but also achieve Eagle Scout, the highest rank in Boy Scouts. Ed said his older son worked hard and never missed a beat despite the severity of his injuries. Peter would go on to attend Rhode Island School of Design and is making a career as a senior designer on the West Coast. Ed, as he says, "is prouder than hell."

It is all a great source of joy for this doting father, but it cannot make him whole. Peter's success and Matthew's accomplishments and continued incremental improvement are a gift, but when it comes to his youngest, they can also be a curse.

"It's the only regret I have in my life," Ed said. "I don't regret things. I obviously regret losing Susan, the injuries to Peter, I regret the whole thing, but the one that faces me every single day is Matthew, and I will never, never get over it. Every day of my life I have to see this child not accomplish what he could accomplish. And that is something Doug Bouch will never get, will never understand."

That sentiment is like a chorus in a song for Ed Slattery; that familiar track in his life he now knows by heart and sometimes feels compelled to belt out. Sometimes, Ed hates Doug Bouch, and he uses the modern day version of singing at the top of his lungs to express the melancholy refrain that defines his struggle. Ed wanted to be heard, and he took to Facebook for infrequent but therapeutic outbursts.

"This day just keeps on giving," Ed wrote on his wall one summer night.

Matthew just fell out of bed onto our concrete floor. Fortunately, his decorative pillows were on the floor and his head fell on them.

Grammar and sentence structure deteriorated from there, like an angry man pounding the keyboard sans his normal measured intellect. Ed began furiously typing fragments as the anger began to build.

Had to pull the opposite side nightstand out, so I could move the bed enough to get between him and his fucking power chair, the one I hate with a passion, to get under his arms. He's now 160 lbs of dead weight.

He's all tucked in with pillows hospital-style. He has a rail on one side, but has never even come close to falling out of bed before. Sleep well, my man.

Walk out of his room to see that the dog shit in the hallway.
You know what? I hate Doug Bouch right this minute. I don't allow myself to hate him, usually, but right now, watching my baby boy, Matthew is the baby, go through seizures, to struggle finding words to tell me what he wants, and struggling to read, unable to walk. Yes, it's getting to me today.

Nearly six years of stress, death, near death, no Susan at graduations, birthdays, weddings, and a seizure finally gets to me. Sorry, folks, but I'm losing it tonight. Feeling anger and even a little hatred. Not proud of it, but there it is.
Let's see if we can get some sleep."

It had been years since the crash, but Matthew was beginning to develop seizures, another hurdle the poor boy couldn't navigate on his own, and it was more than Ed could bear. It was very much that razor's edge he spoke about and, a week later, it sliced him open again.

"Normal busy day," Ed began his post.

At Matthew's pediatrician for Boy Scouts physical, and he goes into a full blown seizure like last week. Vomiting all over me. Lasted about one-and-a-half minutes until postictal phase, which lasted three to four minutes. Back to baseline after forty-five minutes, or so.

Got home, watching Star Wars, maybe not a good idea in retrospect. Another seizure, just like last week. Not as long, but just as much seizing, vomiting, but a little shorter.
Postictal now and resting quietly.

I hate Doug Bouch. He thinks I ruined his life by telling the judge I thought he should go to jail as a deterrent to other truckers who might fall asleep at the wheel. I ruined his life and he took Susan's life and Matthew has to deal with learning to walk, talk, read, do math all over again and now seizures. Asshole!

Angry? Yes I'm angry, but mostly I'm sad and scared. What he did to our little boy is sometimes unbearable. What's his future? More seizures? Brain surgery to treat the seizures? What kind of care does he get when I am no longer here? Who's going to love him like I do?
Son of a bitch!

Despite these public displays, Ed Slattery told me he doesn't really hate Doug Bouch. The man is incapable of hate. But he was angry. Ed's anger had been left unresolved for far too long. It never softened, it never faded. Instead, it blended into the background of his subconscious until something triggered it. Much like Matthew's newfound violent seizures, it was that one-more symptom layered on top of an already-crippling condition that reawakened Ed's anger at Doug Bouch. But this time, it was Ed vomiting hate and angrily and uncontrollably expressing himself against this man who refused to take any responsibility for driving that truck through the middle of his life.

It was energy Ed Slattery needed to expend, and truthfully, in his most vulnerable moments, he knew he'd have to expend more in the future. Resolution from Doug Bouch would never come. It was, is, and always would be the kind of unfinished business that can unsettle the fragile balance Ed worked so hard to build for his reclaimed family. But, while resolution was out of reach, purpose was not. Ed could utilize his anger more constructively by taking action; that Susan's death and Matthew's life didn't have to be in vain. Ed's newfound energy was better spent not only improving his son's life, but those like him. Ed had the power to give, and giving back was the kind of energy that could stave off anger...and he found it on a pornography website.

Ed had always been hyper-focused on making Matthew's life easier. Any tool he could find that promised to eliminate another hurdle of being disabled was ordered, tested, and, ultimately, tossed out in the garbage. None of it was worthy, none of it stood up to the real-life application of disabled life.

This became poignantly clear when Matthew began walking with the assistance of a standard gray walker. As simple as it was, walking stimulated Matthew's brain, and well...his bowels, and that was a great thing. It also accounted for some much-needed exercise, but Ed quickly realized the walker was too light. It was made of aluminum and would easily skirt out from underneath Matthew as he struggled to take steps on the smooth concrete floor of the family's home.

Weights. Ed knew how to solve the problem, he needed weights to attach to the walker to help stabilize his nearly-adult son, as he took his limited steps through the home. Ed tried several solutions, like sandbags, or even ankle weights but they would fall off, or easily shift, throwing off the center of gravity on the walker. It was an adventurous visit on Google that won the day. Ed searched online for circular weights and, innocently enough, stumbled onto sites like thechaingang.com or Lovehoney.com. Yes, the weights used for testicular elongation, or as the site called it, "ball stretching," seemed to be just the remedy Ed needed for Matthew's walker.

For about $50 a pop, these surgical steel ring weights fit on the legs of the walker like a charm. Still, it seemed like a long and, well, undignified way to go for a solution Ed was certain so many other disabled people could use.

Matthew's struggles were becoming Ed's muse; automatic umbrellas for wheelchairs, a collision-avoidance system, a backup camera, even proximity sensors for the visually impaired. It was clear there was a need for things like an automatic device to bring a backpack from behind a wheelchair to the patient's side, or even just a dependable cup holder for a wheelchair. Ed was trying to remove real-life hurdles to the disabled, and the free market, sans the unintentional help of a porn site, was a near-complete void of any useful ideas.

Ed started small by building a prototype for his walker weights. With help, he designed and made two of them with the hope he could eventually market the weights. It was satisfying work, but Ed wanted to do more with more.

If necessity is the mother of invention, then Ed wanted to be the father. He enlisted the help of the Digital Harbor Foundation in downtown Baltimore. Digital Harbor is a non-profit that transformed a closed down city recreation center into a tech center for youth. This technology education ranges from web development, to digital fabrication, electronics, and coding. It was the perfect setting for Ed to introduce his big idea, an "Abilities Hackathon."

A hackathon is what it sounds like, a marathon of hacking or exploratory programming, and Ed wanted these kids to put their tech minds to solving issues disabled people face every day.

It took nine months to put the first one together, but, in the end, there were fifty participants. Some were as young as fourteen, who took second place by programming a video game for an iPhone for visually impaired users. The game worked using audible cues when the character got too close to danger or a wall in a maze. It is an idea that, in its very basic form, could help with Ed's desire for a wheelchair avoidance system.

First place went to a team that developed an audible version of a smartphone app. For example, instead of needing dexterity to use an app, like Uber, the user would simply call on the phone, and it would audibly walk them through the menu. It was called "Tuber."

The "Abilities Hackathon" was a small success, but Ed already has eyes on making it an annual event, where hundreds of youthful designers would tackle the everyday struggles disabled people face each and every day.

But Ed also wanted to change the surroundings of the disabled. Struck by how Matthew's progress quickened as the family moved into their state-of-the-art home, Ed got the idea to start a nonprofit to do the same for others.

Ed became a true believer in the Universal Design concept after building his home in Baltimore County. He pushed the limits of his architects and builders, and the home has been featured in several magazines and features since. Universal Design is producing buildings, products, and environments that are inherently accessible to those both with and without disabilities. While incredibly helpful to those handicapped, it isn't exactly affordable, and it is with that in mind that Ed Slattery began helping other families who faced the same hurdles as his.

This also includes maintaining the fund he started at the Kennedy Krieger Institute in Baltimore where Matthew received the bulk of his therapy and treatment. Ed started with a million dollars but continues to donate every year so that children who need specialized treatment can continue to receive it if their insurance runs out and they have no other means. Ed would like to see more children cared for, and less meatball subs thrown at walls.

It is the kind of work Ed is compelled to do, not out of obligation, rather, out of a duty to do to the right thing. He became a champion of the disabled because he is a champion of Matthew. It is a relationship Ed wanted to use to change the world, or the parts he is lucky enough to be able to touch. His is a cautionary tale, and he has chosen to tell it by using his wealth to help people until, well, it fiscally hurts. But it isn't just money he gives, it is his time.

Ed remains very involved in the Truck Safety Coalition. He lobbies when the group needs him to, he tells his story to personalize the standards it tries to pass in Congress and, perhaps most importantly of all, he lends an ear to new victims from American roadways.

Above all, the Truck Safety Coalition markets itself as a resource for victims of truck crashes throughout the United States, and one of its most powerful tools is Ed Slattery and his family's story.

For Ed, not hearing remorse from the driver, who caused so much carnage in his life, will always echo in the void of resolution. His life, or that chapter of it, still reads like an ellipsis, followed by a blank page. The way he figures it, though, Ed has about another twenty years on this earth and wants to accomplish something and be successful with his third act. With money no longer a qualifier, as it may be for most, he believes he found his true calling in helping others. For Ed Slattery, advocating for other crash victims, the abilities hackathon, and the Slattery Fund at KKI, it really is, and for the rest of his life will be, all about what he can do for others.

Ed continues to lobby for stronger trucking safety regulations. For many reasons, it remains an uphill battle, but as the fatalities from large commercial truck crashes now surge well above four thousand people a year, Ed continues to lend his story to the cause until governmental policies shift.

It is a full-time dedication, but, in doing so, Ed has found a path toward healing his past. His new purpose has allowed him to come full circle, a path blazed by tragedy, but now a journey hardened with purpose and Susan's honor.

It is with that newfound purpose that finally, after nearly six years, Ed was able to slip off his and Susan's rings. His hand felt naked and vulnerable, but altogether lighter. It was as if Susan herself lifted his burden.

Ed decided in that moment that his sons should each have one of the rings. He wrote them a letter explaining why. This was not just some grand gesture, but rather, it was to be his resolution of years of immense pain and loss. His sons needed to hear the words he had written, as this was his last "Dear Susan."

These rings are the tokens of love that Mom and I gave each other on our wedding day. But they are more than just tokens. I don't agree with the idea that a formal marriage is 'just a piece of paper' and 'who needs rings' to proclaim their love to each other. I believe the 'paper' and 'rings' are public statements of love. True, they are not the love, but they proclaim that love to the world. This, I believe has value.

But the real manifestation of your mom's and my love is in you. You are the personifications, the embodiments, literally, of the love we had and have for each other.

So, I don't need these rings anymore, as you are my memory of Mom. It is through my own memories, in my own head, and through the lives that you choose to live, that I will forever honor Susan, your mom.

These now are for you to keep and use as you see fit now and into the future. You may give them to your love, someday, you can have them made into something for yourselves, or just keep them as memories of the love your parents had and have for you.

Mom and I love you both to the ends of the earth and back again.

That will never change.

Estes Express Lines response

Estes Express Lines declined to be interviewed for this book, but the company did send along the following statement:

"Our thoughts and prayers go out to Ed, Matthew, Peter, and their family every day. We will never forget this horrific accident and the lives that were tragically altered that day as a result. While we could not undo what happened, what we could do was to be accountable, to separate the driver [Doug Bouch] from our company, and provide the Slattery's with the financial resources needed to move forward.

We realize that every time one of our drivers is on the road, they have a significant responsibility to themselves and the public. What happened to the Slattery family serves as a constant reminder to drivers that the most important goal is to arrive safely without incident.

Estes remains steadfastly committed to running a safe and responsible operation."

Asked if the company has added any safety measures since the crash that killed Susan Slattery, the company responded that it had implemented both technology and programs to improve driver performance and truck safety including:

- Electronic logs
- Collision Avoidance system
- Lane Departure system
- Sleep Apnea program for identifying and monitoring symptoms of the disorder

- Cameras installed on units to monitor driver behaviors
- Driver Return to Work program to ensure driver readiness following personal illness

Estes says it also now provides driver education, training and safety programs, enforce stringent vehicle maintenance standards and continually research equipment innovation to improve safety.

Acknowledgments

By this point, if you're reading this, I hope it's in an, *I don't want to leave this story or these characters* kind of way. I tried to write a book that stuck with you. This story certainly did for me, and always will. But I didn't do it alone, not even close. There are plenty of people to which I am indebted.

I want to start with Ed and Matthew and the Slattery family. My hope is that you feel like you know them by now and, yes, that is how I feel about them, too. Courage, strength, resilience; it is important to read about people like this. It was selfless for Ed to go public with his story and, as a journalist and now author, I will be forever grateful he chose and believed in me to do it justice. I truly hope I have. I extend a deep thanks to Susan's family as well who, at various points, welcomed me into their home and were quick with a smile when talking about Susan.

To my agent Damian McNicholl, thank you, sir, for believing in the story and your insistence there was an eager audience.

Thank you to Lynn Price, my editor who made this story better with the red pen and keeping it focused right where it needed to be. It's a big book and a timeless tale, she said. Behler Publications believed in this story, and I am grateful.

Personally, this would not have been possible without the support of my parents, Fred and Florence Kuebler. As they tell it, I was nearly left back in kindergarten because, as stubborn as I could be, I refused to read. My mother insisted to the school that I would read and saw to it that I did that summer; although I am not sure she promised them I would become a published author as well. And to my in-laws, Brian and Denise Hein, there is not a better family I could have married into. Your support has been incredible.

To my dear friends Richard and Annabelle (A-belle) Sher...I have so much deep gratitude to you both as you selflessly helped me at every step along this journey while encouraging and believing this story was important enough to be published.

You aren't reading this book and I don't know how to write it without Wayne Freedman. He is the best storyteller in news, period. I was lucky to have been molded early in my career by his incessant insistence on never sacrificing story and the power of the universal truth.

There aren't many better news photographers in Baltimore than Lamont Williams of WMAR 2-News. We shot that first story together, and he visually set its tone not just in an Emmy-award winning television news package, but also in my mind's eye as I wrote this book.

I also don't tell this story without my News Director Kelly Groft. In fact, she insisted on it. I am grateful that she not only assigned me this story back in 2010, but also more importantly, always thought I was the right guy to tell it.

There are tons of others, the good people at the Kennedy Krieger Institute in Baltimore and the staff at the Akron Children's Hospital who never hesitated in granting me the access to tell this tale.

And to my family and friends who always asked after the project or encouraged me along the way: Ami, Mike, Pete, Chele, Stephen, Dan, Rachel, Tony, Chrissy, Marc, Nic, Marissa, and so many more. So. Many. More.

Most importantly, the biggest thank you goes to my wife Tiffany Kuebler who put up with so many *long nights and weekends.* She is my number one cheerleader who always thought this would happen. She never had a doubt, no matter how hard I stubbornly tried to convince her otherwise. Always the measured reason to my emotion, her resolve is the foundation that allows me to achieve big things.

~ Brian Kuebler